MW01054410

MESSIAH

in

Both Testaments

By Fred John Meldau

Editor: CHRISTIAN VICTORY MAGAZINE, Denver, Colo. 80211, U.S.A.

Martino Publishing
Mansfield Centre, CT
2012

Martino Publishing
P.O. Box 373,
Mansfield Centre, CT 06250 USA

www.martinopublishing.com

ISBN   978-1-61427-264-9

© *2012 Martino Publishing*

Cover design by T. Matarazzo

Printed in the United States of America On 100% Acid-Free Paper

MESSIAH

in

Both Testaments

By Fred John Meldau

Editor: CHRISTIAN VICTORY MAGAZINE, Denver, Colo. 80211, U.S.A.

Published, 1956, by
THE CHRISTIAN VICTORY PUBLISHING COMPANY
2909 Umatilla St., Denver, Colo. 80211, U.S.A.
PRINTED IN U.S.A.

CONTENTS

NOTE: The Biblical references in this book for the most part are from the King James, Authorized Version; so we suggest you use an Authorized Version Bible as you look up the references. We use the abbreviation RV to indicate the Revised Version — the American Standard Revised of 1901.

The Greatest Miracle in Print: the Record of

MESSIAH in Both Testaments

"To HIM give all the prophets witness" (Acts 10:43). "In the volume of the Book it is written of Me" (Ps. 40:7; Heb. 10:7).

INTRODUCTION

"THE MOST AMAZING DRAMA that ever was presented to the mind of man—a drama written in prophecy in the Old Testament and in biography in the four Gospels—is the narrative of Jesus the Christ. One outstanding fact, among many, completely isolates HIM. It is this: that one Man only in the history of the world has had explicit details given beforehand of His birth, life, death and resurrection; that these details are in documents given to the public centuries before He appeared, and that no one challenges, or can challenge, that these documents were widely circulated long before His birth; and that anyone and everyone can compare for himself the actual records of His life with those old documents, and find that they match one another to a nicety. The challenge of this pure miracle is that it happened concerning one Man only in the whole history of the world" (D. M. Panton).*

To focus attention on the unparalleled wonder of this literary miracle, think for a moment: who could have prewritten a life of George Washington or Abraham Lincoln, or any other

---

*Scores of other Bible students have called attention to this same amazing fact. We quote from one more, Canon Dyson Hague. He says: "Centuries before Christ was born His birth and career, His sufferings and glory, were all described in outline and detail in the Old Testament. Christ is the only Person ever born into this world whose ancestry, birthtime, forerunner, birth-place, birth-manner, infancy, manhood, teaching, character, career, preaching, reception, rejection, death, burial, resurrection and ascension were all prewritten in the most marvelous manner centuries before He was born.

"Who could draw a picture of a man not yet born? Surely God, and God alone. Nobody knew 500 years ago that Shakespeare was going to be born; or 250 years ago that Napoleon was to be born. Yet here in the Bible we have the most striking and unmistakable likeness of a Man portrayed, not by one, but by twenty or twenty-five artists, none of whom had ever seen the Man they were painting."

character, five hundred years before he was born? No where in any of the literature of the world, secular or religious, can one find a duplicate to the astounding miracle of the pre-written life of Christ. "The inspiration of that portrait came from the Heavenly Gallery, and not from the studio of an earthly artist" (A. T. Pierson). So amazing is this miracle of the pre-written life of Christ and its perfect fulfillment in Jesus of Nazareth that "Nothing but Divine prescience could have foreseen it, and nothing but Divine power could accomplish it." As the full evidence is presented, all thoughtful readers will agree that "the prophecy came not in old time by the will of man, but holy men of God spake as they were moved by the Holy Spirit" (2 Pet. 1:21).

Four Great Truths Demonstrated by This Fact

With no variations or aberrations between the Old Testament predictions of the coming Messiah and the New Testament fulfillment in Jesus of Nazareth, one instinctively leaps to the conclusion that "the Hand that drew the Image in prophecy moulded the Portrait in history"; and the inevitable conclusion to this miracle is fourfold:

(1) It proves that the Bible is the inspired Word of God, for unaided man is neither capable of writing nor fulfilling such a literary wonder.

(2) It proves that the God of the Bible, the only One who knows the end from the beginning, and who alone has the power to fulfill all His word, is the true and living God.

(3) It demonstrates that the God of the Bible is both all-knowing to be able to foretell the future entwined around numberless men who are free moral agents, and all-powerful, to be able to bring to pass a perfect fulfillment of His word in the midst of widespread unbelief, ignorance and rebellion on the part of men.

(4) It demonstrates that the Person, Jesus of Nazareth, who so perfectly and completely fulfilled all the Old Testament predictions is indeed the Messiah, the Saviour of the world, the Son of the Living God.

Christ Is the Center of History

So CHRIST is seen to be the center of all history as well as the central theme of the Bible. "The Christ of the New Testament is the fruit of the tree of prophecy, and Christianity is the realization of a plan, the first outlines of which were sketched more than 1500 years before."*

*David Baron, in Rays of Messiah's Glory, p. 14.

Fulfilled Prophecy Is Unique to the Bible

The fact of fulfilled prophecy is found in the Bible alone; hence, it presents proof of Divine inspiration that is positive, conclusive, overwhelming. Here is the argument in brief: no man, unaided by Divine inspiration, foreknows the future, for it is an impenetrable wall, a true "iron curtain," to all mankind. Only an almighty and an all-knowing God can infallibly predict the future. If then one can find true prophecy (as one does in the Bible), with definite fulfillment, with sufficient time intervening between the prediction and the fulfillment, and with explicit details in the prediction to assure that the prophecies are not clever guesses, then the case is perfect and unanswerable. Remember, there were 400 years between the last of the Messianic predictions of the Old Testament and their fulfillment in the Christ of the Gospels.* Many prophecies are of course much older than 400 B. C. During the period of 1100 years, from the age of Moses (1500 B.C.) to that of Malachi (400 B.C.), a succession of prophets arose, Messianic prediction took form, and all of them testified of the Messiah who was to come.

So minute and so voluminous are these Old Testament predictions and so complete is their fulfillment in the New Testament, that Dr. A. T. Pierson says, "There would be no honest infidel in the world were Messianic prophecy studied . . . nor would there be any doubting disciples if this fact of predic-

---

*The perfect proof of the long period of time that elapsed between the last book of the Old Testament and the first book of the New Testament is the presence in the world of the SEPTUAGINT, a translation of the Old Testament into Greek about 200 B.C. This translation was begun in the reign of Ptolemy Philadelphus, about 280 B.C. and was completed not long after. With a TRANSLATION of the entire Old Testament, as we now know it, made over 200 years B.C., it is obvious that the books of the Old Testament from which the translation was made are still older.

It is well to remember also that there were no prophets in the 400-year inter-testament period. In 1 Macc. 9:27 we are told of the "great affliction in Israel, such as there was not since the day that a prophet was not seen among them." Intense regret over the lack of a prophet merged into an intense longing for the coming again of prophets, so that even in their public actions men were careful to claim validity for their legislation only until a faithful prophet should again rise. (See 1 Macc. 14:41; 4:46.)

tion and fulfillment were fully understood." "And," he continues, "the sad fact is, we have yet to meet the first honest skeptic or critic who has carefully studied the prophecies which center in Christ" (Many Infallible Proofs). Here indeed is "God's Rock of Ages, faith's unshakable standing place."

"Prophecy" Is God's Own Method of Proving His Truth

The teachings of the Bible are so peculiar and different from all other religions, and so important—telling us that man's eternal destiny, for weal or woe, depends on his acceptance of the Christ of the Bible—that we have the right to **know** whether the Bible is or is not a Heavenly Decree, the absolute and final Word of God, whether its message is fully authorized by the Almighty. If God **has** given a revelation of His will in the Bible, there can be no doubt that in some unmistakable way He will show men that the Bible is indeed His revealed will; and the way He has chosen to show men that the Bible is His Word is a way that all men of average intelligence can understand; and that way is through the giving and through the fulfillment of specific, detailed prophecies. It is the Divine seal, letting all men know that He has spoken. This seal can never be counterfeited, affixed to the Truth which it attests—for His foreknowledge of the actions of free and intelligent agents, men, is one of the most "incomprehensible attributes of Deity and is exclusively a Divine perfection."*

In challenging the false gods of Isaiah's time, the true God said:

"Produce your cause . . . bring forth your strong reasons . . . show us what shall happen . . . declare us things for to come. Show us things that are to come hereafter, that we may know that ye are gods" (Isa. 41:21-23).

There are false faiths like Mohammedanism and Buddhism that have tried to prop up their claims on pretended miracles, but neither these, nor any other religion in the history of the world. except the Bible, have ever ventured to frame prophecies.

It is the peculiar "glory" of the Almighty, the all-knowing God, who is "the Lord, the Creator" (Isa. 40:28) to "declare

---

*Evidences of Prophecy, by Alexander Keith; p. 8.

new things before they spring forth" (Isa. 42:8-9) and that glory He will not share with another (Isa. 42:8). The true God alone foreknows and foretells the future. And He has chosen to confine his foretelling to the pages of Scripture."* Though there are many other subjects of Divine Prophecy in the Bible—such as the Jews, the Gentile nations that surrounded Israel, ancient cities, the Church, the last days, etc., the divine perfections of foreknowledge and fulfillment can be seen better in the realm of prophecies concerning Christ than in any other sphere.

Here is the clear statement that God alone, in the Bible alone, gave true prophecies:

"I am God, and there is none else; I am God, and there is none like Me, DECLARING THE END FROM THE BEGINNING, and from ancient times the things that are not yet done, saying, MY COUNSEL SHALL STAND AND I WILL DO ALL MY PLEASURE" (Isa. 45:9, 10). (The appeal by God that He alone can give and fulfill prophecy, and that it is to be found alone in the Bible, is found in many places in the Bible. See 2 Timothy 3:16; 2 Peter 1:19-21; Deuteronomy 18:21, 22; Isaiah 41:21-23; Jeremiah 28:9; John 13:19, etc.)

Sensing the tremendous force of this fact, Justin Martyr said, "To declare a thing shall come to pass long before it is in being, and to bring it to pass, this or nothing is the work of God."

"Chance Fulfillment" of Prophecy Is Ruled Out

Desperate atheists and other unbelievers, seeking a way to

---

*Many have made an effort to foretell the future—not one, outside the Bible, has ever succeeded. "The extreme difficulty of framing a prophecy which shall prove accurate, may be seen in that familiar but crude rhyme known as 'Mother Shipton's Prophecy'. Some years ago it appeared as a pretended relic of a remote day, and claimed to have predicted the invention of the steam locomotive, the rise of D'Israeli in English politics, etc., etc. . . . For years I tried to unearth and expose what seemed to me a huge imposture, and I succeeded. . . . I traced the whole thing to one Charles Hindley (of England) who acknowledged himself the author of this prophetic hoax, which was written in 1862 instead of 1448, and palmed off on a credulous public. It is one of the startling proofs of human perversity that the very people who will try to cast suspicion on prophecies two thousand years old, will, without straining, swallow a forgery that was first published AFTER the events it predicted, and will not even look into its claim to antiquity." (Dr. A. T. Pierson, pp. 44, 45, in Many Infallible Proofs.)

circumvent the fact of fulfilled prophecy and its connotations, have argued that the fulfillments were "accidental," "chance," or "co-incidental." But when a number of details are given the "chance" fulfillment of prophecy is ruled out. One writer says, "It is conceivable that a prediction, uttered at a venture and expressing what in a general way may happen to resume may seem like a genuine prophecy. But only let the prophecy give several DETAILS of time, place and accompanying incidents and it is evident that the possibility of a chance fulfillment, by a 'fortuitous concurrence of events,' will become extremely desperate—yea, altogether impossible. Hence the prophecies of heathen antiquity always took good care to confine their predictions to one or two particulars and to express them in the most general and ambiguous terms. Therefore, in the whole range of history, except the prophecies of Scripture, there is not a single instance of a prediction, expressed in unequivocal language, and descending to any minuteness, which bears the slightest claim to fulfillment. 'Suppose,' says Dr. Olinthus Gregory, 'that there were only 50 prophecies in the Old Testament (instead of 333) concerning the first advent of Christ, giving details of the coming Messiah and all meet in the person of Jesus . . . the probability of chance fulfillment as calculated by mathematicians according to the theory of probabilities, is less than one in 1,125,000,000,000,000. Now add only two more elements to these 50 prophecies, and fix the TIME and the PLACE at which they must happen and the immense improbability that they will take place by chance exceeds all the power of numbers to express (or the mind of man to grasp). This is enough, one would think, to silence for ever all pleas for chance as furnishing an unbeliever the least opportunity of escape from the evidence of prophecy.' (Gregory's Letters)."*

Let it be further observed that many of the prophecies about Messiah are of such a nature that only God could fulfill them, such as His virgin birth, His sinless and holy character, His resurrection and His ascension. Only GOD could cause Jesus "to be born of a virgin or be raised from the dead" (David Baron).

---

*Evidences of Prophecy, by Alexander Keith; p. 8.

THE COMING MESSIAH

IN THE OLD TESTAMENT there is a definite, clear and continuous teaching that "Messiah will come." Dozens of times we read such promises as "Behold **thy King cometh** unto thee" (Zech. 9:9); "the Lord God will come" (Isa. 40:10); "the Lord, whom ye seek, shall suddenly come to His temple" (Mal. 3:1); "the Lord thy God will raise up unto thee a Prophet from the midst of thee" (Deut. 18:15-19) who will be the Lord's "fellow" (equal) (Zech. 13:7). Daniel predicted the coming of "Messiah the Prince" at a set time (Dan. 9:25, 26), and Isaiah foretold of the "rod out of the stem of Jesse" (Isa. 11:1) on whom the Lord would "lay the iniquity of us all" (Isa. 53). Prophets and Seers of old often spoke of the time when "the Desire of all Nations" would come (Hag. 2:7). (See also Isa. 35:4; Gen. 49:10; Num. 24:37; Ps. 118:26; Ps. 2:5-6; Jerem. 23:5-6; Isa. 62:11; Gen. 3:15, etc.).

Christ's Coming Is the Central Theme of the Bible

The coming of Christ, promised in the Old Testament and fulfilled in the New—His birth, character, work, teachings, His sufferings, death and resurrection—are the grand, central themes of the Bible. Christ is the bond that ties the two Testaments together. The Old Testament is in the New revealed, the New Testament is in the Old concealed.

The Average Bible Reader Can Understand

"The most ordinary reader," says A. T. Pierson, "may examine the old curious predictions of the Messiah's person and work found in the Old Testament, follow the gradual progress of these revelations from Genesis to Malachi, and trace the prophecies as they descend into details more and more specific and minute, until at last the full figure of the Coming One stands out. Then, with this image clearly fixed in his mind's eye, he may turn to the New Testament and beginning with Matthew, see how the **historic** personage, Jesus of Nazareth, corresponds and coincides in every particular with the **prophetic** personage depicted by the prophets. . . . There is not a difference or a divergence, yet there could have been no collusion or contact between the prophets of the Old Testament and the narrators of the New Testament. Observe, **the reader** has not gone out of the Bible itself. He has simply compared two portraits; one in the Old Testament of a mysterious Coming one, another is in the New of One who has actually come; and his irresistible conclusion is that these two blend in absolute unity."

A BRIEF SUMMARY OF THE PROPHECIES

Let us briefly trace a few of the outstanding points in the comparison of Old Testament prediction and New Testament fulfillment. The work of redemption was to be accomplished by One Person, the Central figure in both Testaments, the promised Messiah. As the "Seed of the woman" (Gen. 3:15) He was to bruise Satan's head (Gal. 4:4). As the "Seed of Abraham" (Gen. 22:18 with Gal. 3:16) and the "Seed of David" (Ps. 132:11; Jerem. 23:5 with Acts 13:23) He was to come from the tribe of Judah (Gen. 49:10 with Heb. 7:14).

He must come at a specified time (Gen. 49:10; Dan. 9:24-25 with Luke 2:1), be born of a virgin (Isa. 7:14 with Matt. 1:18-23), at Bethlehem of Judea (Mic. 5:2 with Matt. 2:1; Luke 2:5, 6). Great persons were to visit and adore Him (Ps. 72:10 with Matt. 2:1-11). Through the rage of a jealous king, innocent children were to be slaughtered (Jerem. 31:15 with Matt. 2:16-18).

He was to be preceded by a forerunner, John the Baptist, before entering His public ministry (Isa. 40:3; Mal. 3:1 with Luke 1:17 and Matt. 3:1-3).

He was to be a prophet like Moses (Deut. 18:18 with Acts 3:20-22); have a special anointing of the Holy Spirit (Ps. 45:7; Isa. 11:2; Isa. 61:1, 2 with Matt. 3:16; Luke 4:15-21, 43). He was to be a priest after the order of Melchizedeck (Ps. 110:4 with Heb. 5:5, 6). As the "Servant of the Lord" He was to be a faithful and patient Redeemer, for the Gentiles as well as the Jews (Isa. 42:1-4 with Matt. 12:18-21).

His ministry was to begin in Galilee (Isa. 9:1,2 with Matt. 4:12, 16-23); later, He was to enter Jerusalem (Zech. 9:9 with Matt. 21:1-5) to bring salvation. He was to enter the temple (Hag. 2:7-9; Mal. 3:1 with Matt. 21:12).

His zeal for the Lord is spoken of (Ps. 69:9 with John 2:17). His manner of teaching was to be by parables (Ps. 78:2 with Matt. 13:34-35); and His ministry was to be characterized by miracles (Isa. 35:5-6 with Matt. 11:4-6, John 11:47). He was to be rejected by His brethren (Ps. 69:8, Isa. 53:3 with John 1:11, John 7:5) and be a "Stone of stumbling" to the Jews and a "Rock of offense" (Isa. 8:14 with Rom. 9:32, 1 Pet. 2:8).

He was to be hated without a cause (Ps. 69:4; Isa. 49:7 with John 7:48; John 15:25), rejected by the rulers (Ps. 118:22 with Matt. 21:42, John 7:48), betrayed by a friend (Ps. 41:9; Ps. 55: 12, 14 with John 13: 18, 21), forsaken by His disciples (Zech. 13:7 with Matt. 26:31-56), sold for 30 pieces of silver (Zech. 11:12 with Matt. 26:15) and His price given for the potter's field (Zech. 11:13 with Matt. 27:7), smitten on the cheek (Mic. 5:1 with Matt. 27:30), spat on (Isa. 50:6 with Matt. 27:30), mocked (Ps. 22:7-8 with Matt. 27:31, 39-44) and beaten (Ps. 50:6f.c. with Matt. 26:67; 27:26,30).*

His death by crucifixion is given in detail in Psalm 22; and the **meaning** of His death, as a substitutionary atonement, is given in Isaiah 53. His hands and His feet were to be pierced (Ps. 22:16; Zech. 12:10 with John 19:18; John 19:37 and John 20:25); yet, not a bone of Him was to be broken (Exod. 12:46; Ps. 34:20 with John 19:33-36). He was to suffer thirst (Ps. 22:15 with John 19:28) and be given vinegar to drink (Ps. 69:21 with Matt. 27:34); and He was to be numbered with transgressors (Isa. 53:12 with Matt. 27:38).

His body was to be buried with the rich in His death (Isa. 53:9 with Matt. 27:57-60), but was not to see corruption (Ps. 16:10 with Acts 2:31).

He was to be raised from the dead (Ps. 2:7; 16:10 with Acts 13:33), ascend to the right hand of God (Ps. 68:18 with Luke 24:51; Acts 1:9; also Ps. 110:1 with Heb. 1:3).

This bare sketch of Old Testament Messianic prophecy with its New Testament fulfillment is of course far from complete;

---

*It is most impressive to read in parallel statements the prediction in comparison with the fulfillment. For example, compare Isaiah 50:6 with the New Testament fulfillment:

Prophecy: "I gave my back to the smiters, and my cheeks to them that plucked off the hair; I hid not my face from shame and spitting."

Fulfillment: "Then did they spit in His face and buffeted Him; and others smote Him with the palms of their hands" (Matt. 26:67).

it is merely suggestive, though we have covered many of the main points. Remember, there are actually 333 predictions concerning the Coming Messiah in the Old Testament!**

THE MESSIAH WHO HAS COME

Christ's Testimony to the Fact That He Fulfilled Old Testament Prophecy

The Golden Milestone in the ancient city of Rome, was the point in the old world at which the many roads, running from all directions in the Roman Empire, met and converged. So all lines of Old Testament Messianic prophecy meet in Jesus the Christ of the New Testament.

Not only was the life of Christ prewritten in the Old Testament, but Jesus the Christ of the New Testament knew it and fully witnessed to that fact in the New Testament. This is a miracle in itself, and finds no parallel in the literature of the world. No other character of history—Caesar, Gladstone, Shakespeare, or any other—ever dreamed of saying of the Bible or any other book, as our Lord did, "Search the Scriptures, for they . . . testify of Me" (John 5:39). Nor has any false Christ ever appealed to fulfilled prophecy to vindicate his claims.*

So we face this vast truth: Christianity is NOT a new religion unconnected with the Old Testament. It is based solidly on being the **fulfillment** of Old Testament promises. "Chris-

---

**It is valuable however to gather together as in a great museum at least some of the prophetic masterpieces scattered throughout the realm of the entire 39 books of the Old Testament, so that the reader can get a view of them in one group without having to travel laboriously throughout the hundreds of pages of the Scriptures.

*In "Rays of Messiah's Glory," page 46, David Baron calls attention to the fact that "More than forty false Messiahs have appeared in the history of the Jewish nation," and NOT ONE OF THEM ever appealed to fulfilled prophecy to establish his claims. Rather, they bolstered their fake claims by "promises of revenge and by flatteries which gratified national vanity. And now, except to a few students of history, the remembrance of their names has perished from the earth, while Jesus of Nazareth, the true Messiah, who fulfilled ALL the prophecies, is worshipped by hundreds of millions."

tianity, with its central Figure human and Divine: Prophet, Priest and King, is nothing less than the translation of prophecy from the region of ardent belief to actual fact . . . and we see the living and organic connection between the two Dispensations and recognize it is the same God who spake in both—in the first to prepare, in the second to accomplish. . . . 'Known unto God are all His works from the beginning.' "**

Jesus calmly said, "Abraham saw My day" (John 8:56) and "Moses wrote of Me" (John 5:46). Then, to show the connection between Old Testament prediction and New Testament fulfillment, He said in His Sermon on the Mount, 'I am not come to destroy the law and the prophets . . . but to fulfill them" (Matt. 5:17).

The life of Christ was unique: all was according to the Divine Pattern as given in the Old Testament. He was the "One sent" by the Father to fulfill all His will: to accomplish His work as Redeemer and to fulfill all the prophecies concerning Him (John 3:16, 17; 1 John 4:14; Heb. 10:9).

In the beginning of His ministry, after reading to the people in the synagogue at Capernaum the important Messianic prophecy in Isaiah 61:1,2—when all eyes were fastened on Him—He said, "This day is this Scripture fulfilled in your ears" (Luke 4:16-21). When talking to Him at the well, the woman of Samaria said to Jesus, "I know that Messiah cometh"—all devout readers of the Old Testament knew that—"and when He is come, He will tell us all things." Then the Lord Jesus said to her, "I that speak unto thee am He" (John 4:25, 26). When Peter confessed his faith in Jesus as the Messiah—"Thou art the Christ, the Son of the living God" (Matt. 16:16)— the Lord Jesus acknowledged the truth of what he had said by answering, "Blessed art thou, Simon Bar-Jonah: for flesh and blood hath not revealed it unto thee, but my Father who is in heaven (hath revealed it unto thee)" (Matt. 16:17).

He quoted from Psalm 110 to identify Himself as "Son of David"—a Messianic title—and also to prove that David called Him Lord (Matt. 22:41-46). By taking the title "Son of Man" He identified Himself with that Messianic title as used in Dan-

---

**E. A. Edghill, in The Value of Prophecy, pp. 389, 390.

iel (Dan. 7:13 with Mark 14:62; cf. also Ps. 8). By taking the title "Son of God" He identified Himself with that Messianic title as used in the Second Psalm.

He connected the blessings of salvation given to all who trust in Him with the promises of the Old Testament: "He that believeth on Me, **as the Scripture hath said,** from within him shall flow rivers of living water" (John 7:38 P.V). **Here** our Lord was speaking of the fulfillment, **through Him, of the** type in the Feast of Tabernacles (see context, John 7:37; Lev. 23:34-36; cf. Isa. 12:3).

Almost everything Christ said or did had some connection with Old Testament prophecy. His miracles were in fulfillment of Old Testament predictions (Isa. 35:5, 6); His ministry was in accord with what Isaiah had predicted concerning Him (Isa. 61:1-3; Isa. 42:1-4; cf. Matt. 12:17-21). His sufferings and death at Jerusalem were all in accordance with what had been foretold (Ps. 22; Isa. 53). When praising John the Baptist, Christ called attention to the fact that John was His forerunner, even as was predicted in Isaiah 40:3 and Malachi 3:1.

"For this is he (John the Baptist) of whom it is written, Behold, I send My messenger before thy face, which shall prepare thy way before thee" (Matt. 11:10).

And so, our Lord not only said that **John** came in fulfillment of prophecy, but that He, Jesus, was the One that John came to be Forerunner for!

As he drew near to the cross, He said to His disciples, "Behold, we go up to Jerusalem and **all things that are written by the prophets concerning the Son of man shall be accomplished"** (Luke 18:31). On the eve of His crucifixion, He said, "this which is written **must** be fulfilled in Me, and He was reckoned with transgressor: for **that which concerneth Me hath fulfillment"** (Luke 22:37 RV). Note the word **"must."**

During the crucial hours of His trial, Jesus said to Peter (who was willing to defend his Master with his sword), "Thinkest thou that I cannot now pray to my Father, and He shall even now send Me twelve legions of angels? **But how then shall the Scripture be fulfilled that thus it must be?"** (Matt. 26:55-56). Then chiding the multitudes, He said, "Are ye come out as against a robber with swords and staves to seize

Me? . . . **But all this is come to pass that the Scriptures of the prophets might be fulfilled**" (Matt. 26:55-56). At His trial, when the high priest put Him under oath, and asked Him, "Art thou the Christ, the Son of the Blessed?" Jesus answered, "I AM" (Mark. 14:60-62).

Suffering on the cross, the Lord Jesus identified Himself as the One whose hands and feet were to be pierced (Ps. 22:16), according to Psalm 22, by quoting verse 1 of that Psalm: "My God, my God, why hast thou forsaken Me?" Three of His seven sayings on the cross were in the very words of Scripture.

After His resurrection, while talking to His two disciples on the Emmaus road, He began "at Moses and all the prophets . . . and expounded unto them **in all the Scriptures the things concerning Himself**" (Luke 24: 27). And later, when meeting with the assembled disciples, He said to them, "These are the words which I spake unto you . . . that **all things** MUST **be fulfilled,** which were written in the law of Moses, and in the prophets, and in the Psalms, concerning Me" (Luke 24:44). Notice how the Lord on different occasions spoke of the necessity—"MUST"—of Old Testament prophecy being fulfilled in Him: necessary, because the Word of God cannot fail, and the God of the Word cannot lie, and the Son of God who fulfilled the Word cannot fail. "The Scripture **cannot** be broken" (John 10:35).

The Lord also gave His disciples, after His resurrction, the KEY that unlocks Messianic prophecy in the Old Testament: "And He said unto them, Thus it is written, and thus it behoved Christ to **suffer,** and to rise from the dead the third day (and so He began His 'glory'): and that repentance and remission of sins should be preached in His Name among all nations" (Luke 24:46-47). This great statement is perhaps a summary of His teachings during the forty days that He ministered to His disciples between His resurrection and His ascension. The Jews of His day, and to this day, looked for a triumphant, reigning Messiah, and failed to see from their own Scriptures that Christ must SUFFER for the sins of the people before entering His glory. Peter bears the same testimony of the witness of the Holy Spirit, through the prophets of the Old Testament, when He testified beforehand of "the sufferings of Christ, and the glory that should follow" (1 Peter 1:11).

The Apostles and Writers of the New Testament Also Bear Witness that Jesus the Christ Fulfilled Old Testament Prophecies

Many modern Christians have lost—or never had—an enlightened understanding of the genius of Christianity: that the New Testament is the fulfillment of the predictions and promises of the Old; that Jesus the Christ is the link who binds the two Testaments together. The early New Testament church writers and preachers saw this clearly and constantly pointed out the new Testament fulfillment of Old Testament prophecy.

When Matthew narrated the virgin birth of Christ in Matthew 1:18-25 he said it was the fulfillment of the Old Testament prediction of Messiah's virgin birth:

"Now all this was done, that it might be fulfilled which was spoken of the Lord by the prophet, saying, Behold, a virgin shall be with child, and shall bring forth a son, and they shall call his name Emmanuel, which being interpreted is, God with us" (Matt. 1:22-23; cf. Isa. 7:14).

When King Herod in a jealous rage slaughtered the innocent children in his vain effort to kill the Christ Child, Matthew called attention to the fact that even this gruesome murder was foreknown by God who had it written down in the Bible as a prediction that was then fulfilled (cf. Matthew 2:16-18 with Jerem. 31:15).

In dozens of places in the Gospels the evangelists infer or state that Jesus fulfilled Old Testament prophecy. Peter expressed the convictions of the other disciples when he made his great confession:

"Thou art the Christ, the Son of the living God" (Matthew 16:16). See also Matt. 8:17; 12:17; etc.

It is neither practical nor necessary in this brief treatise to list every case in the New Testament where the writers referred to the fulfillment of some Old Testament prediction. But we do want to call attention to the fact that the **main theme,** not only of the Gospel of John, as stated in John 20:31, but of ALL FOUR GOSPELS, is to prove that Jesus of Nazareth is the predicted Messiah, the Son of God, the One who was to come.

"These are written, that ye might believe that Jesus is the Christ, the Son of God; and that believing ye might have life through His name" (John 20:31).

Paraphrased, this statement reads:

"The Gospel of John was written to offer full proof, so that you might believe it, that Jesus of Nazareth is the Messiah that the Old Testament predicted would come, and this Messiah, this Jesus, is the Son of God. Moreover, you get eternal life through believing on Him."

The gist of John's proof in his Gospel of John is to show that Jesus has all the qualifications, the character, and the works of Messiah—Jesus fulfills all that was written of Messiah—hence He is Messiah.*

The backbone of Peter's sermon on the day of Pentecost was an argument from the Old Testament to prove to the Jews that Jesus of Nazareth, whom they with wicked hands had crucified, but whom God had raised from the dead, was the Messiah that David had written about. And that "this Jesus . . . God raise up . . . and made both Lord and Christ" (Acts 2:22-36).

In Peter's second sermon in the book of Acts (Acts 3:12-26) at the gate of the Temple, he climaxed and enforced his argument and appeal by saying:

"And now brethren, I know that through ignorance ye did it (rejected and killed Jesus, their Messiah), as did also your rulers.

But those things, which God before had showed by the mouth of all His prophets, that Christ should suffer, He hath so fulfilled.

Repent ye therefore, and be converted, that your sins may be blotted out . . ." (Acts 3:17-19).

Even in his sermon to the assembled Gentiles in the house of Cornelius, Peter said,

---

*All the apostles "laid great stress upon this argument from prophecy: it was not only the main, but almost the sole, argument employed in the New Testament . . . (They felt) it necessary to show the marvelous correspondence between the well known facts (of the life, death and resurrection of Christ) with Old Testament prophecy, in order to carry conviction to every fair mind; and so this was the common method of preaching the Gospel, the solid but simple base of argument upon which rested all appeal." (A. T. Pierson, in Many Infallible Proofs; p. 187).

"To Him (Jesus) give all the prophets witness, that through His name whosoever believeth in Him shall receive remission of sins" (Acts 10:43).

In Paul's sermon in the Synagogue at Antioch he said:

"And when they had fulfilled ALL that was written of Him, they took Him down from the tree and laid Him in a sepulchre. But God raised Him from the dead" (Acts 13:29-30).

Paul's method of preaching the Gospel to the Jews is given in Acts 17:2-3:

"And Paul, as his manner was, . . . reasoned with them out of the Scriptures (Old Testament), opening and alleging, that Christ (Messiah) must needs have suffered, and risen again from the dead; and that THIS JESUS, whom I preach unto you, IS CHRIST."

When Paul would define the Gospel, by which people are saved, he connects the New Testament facts of the death and resurrection of Christ, with Old Testament prediction and teaching.

"Moreover, brethren, I declare unto you the gospel . . . by which also ye are saved . . . how that Christ died for our sins ACCORDING TO THE SCRIPTURES (the Old Testament); and that He was buried, and that He rose again the third day ACCORDING TO THE SCRIPTURES" (1 Cor. 15:1-4).

Many more citations could be given to show that the apostles, writers and preachers of the New Testament constantly pointed out that Jesus the Christ lived, suffered, died and rose again in fulfillment of Old Testament prophecy. Commenting on this fact, Dr. A. T. Pierson said, "No miracle which He wrought so unmistakably set on Jesus the seal of God as the convergence of the thousand lines of prophecy in Him, as in one burning focal point of dazzling glory. Every sacrifice presented, from the hour of Abel's altar-fire down to the last passover lamb of the passion week, pointed as with flaming finger to Calvary's cross. Nay, all the centuries moved as in solemn procession to lay their tributes upon Golgotha."

We must now go into more detail, under different categories, to further demonstrate that "all Messianic predictions of the Old Testament converge in Jesus of Nazareth into a focal point of dazzling glory." We will present a brief of the voluminous material under these seven headings:

I. THE CREDENTIALS OF MESSIAH

II. PROPHECIES CONCERNING THE LIFE AND MINISTRY OF MESSIAH

III. PROPHETIC PARADOXES

IV. PROPHECIES CONCERNING THE SUFFERINGS, DEATH AND RESURRECTION OF CHRIST

V. PROPHECIES DESCRIBING THE MESSIANIC OFFICES OF CHRIST

VI. PROPHECIES SHOWING THAT MESSIAH—CHRIST—IS GOD

VII. TYPES AND INDIRECT PROPHECIES OF THE OLD TESTAMENT FULFILLED IN CHRIST

I. THE CREDENTIALS OF MESSIAH

Credentials are testimonials, written proofs, such as letters of commendation, or legal documents, proving the bearer to right of office or position, such as an ambassador brings from his government to a foreign court. Our gracious Redeemer, when He came to our earth, condescended to present His "credentials" from the Heavenly Court. The following facts are the credentials that Jesus is the Christ. Matthew in his first chapter presents a succinct summary of His credentials:

"The book of the generation of Jesus Christ, the son of David, the son of Abraham" (Matt. 1:1).

Reaching One Person Out of a World of People Via Mail

All are familiar with this commonplace fact: any person living in any part of the world having mail service can be picked out from the rest of the three and one-half billion people on earth by simply addressing a letter to him, using six or seven definite specifications. For example, if we write a letter to

LESTER B. SMITH,
　　4143 Madison Ave.,
　　　Chicago, Ill.,
　　　　USA.

we are picking out **one man** from all the world. We can positively identify him and reach him by selecting **one** country where he lives from all the nations of the world—the USA; and so we eliminate all other countries. By selecting **one** state out of the country where he lives—Illinois—we eliminate all other states in the world. By designating **one** city—Chicago— in that state we eliminate all the other cities of the world. By pointing out by the correct address, the **one** house in Chicago where he lives—4143 Madison Ave.—we automatically exclude all other houses of the world, and by **giving him his one** correct name—Lester B. Smith—we not only distinguish him from other individuals who may live in the same house, we also eliminate all other persons in the world!

In like manner, in giving a sufficient number of definite "specifications" in the Old Testament, concerning the coming Messiah, God enabled us to pick out one Man from all history, from all nations, from all peoples, and be absolutely sure that one Man is the Messiah! Let us carefully examine His "credentials," His "address" as it were. These details, these specifications, these elements of His "address," were given that all might know who the true Messiah is. As we proceed with the listing and explanation of these predictions—and their cumulative effect is overwhelming—it will soon become obvious that no other person in all the history of the world could fulfill all the Messianic predictions—or even a very small percentage of them—except JESUS OF NAZARETH.

(1) In the first place, God eliminated **half** of the human race as the immediate parent of Messiah—and at the same time He made it clear Messiah would come as a Man and not as an angel, when He gave the promise that the coming Deliverer would be **"the Seed of the woman."**

"I will put enmity between thee and the woman, and between thy seed and her seed; it shall bruise thy head, and thou shalt bruise his heel" (Gen. 3:15).

This, the first of the direct Messianic promises in the Bible, is "the Bible in embryo, the sum of all history and prophecy in a germ."* For here we have intimated not only the virgin birth of Christ, but also His vicarious sufferings—"thou shalt bruise His heel"—and His complete, eventual victory over Satan and his works—"it (Messiah) shall bruise thy head."

We have remarkable evidence in Genesis 4:1 that this promise in Genesis 3:15 was well understood by Adam and Eve: for at the birth of her first son, Eve ecstatically exclaimed, "I have obtained the Man, even the Lord!" (Heb. of Gen. 4:1). When her firstborn arrived, Eve thought the promised Deliverer had come. But she was mistaken as to the time, place and many other yet-to-be-given specifications. Many centuries must pass before Messiah could come. But when the fulness

---

*H. Grattan Guinness, in The Approaching End of the Age.

of time was come, "God sent forth His Son, **made of a woman** . . . to redeem . . ." (Gal. 4:4).

(2) Next, God eliminated two-thirds of the nations, by indicating that Messiah must come through **Shem**—not Ham or Japheth—of the sons of Noah. In the very beginning of the history of the nations God through His prophet Noah identified Himself with Shem in an especial way:

"Blessed be Jehovah, the God of Shem" (Gen. 9:26 RV).

In the Hebrew of verse 27 there is no word answering to "he" that is found in the AV. So the verse correctly reads:

"God will enlarge Japheth, and will dwell in the tents of Shem" (Gen. 9:27).

The Chaldee of Onkelos thus paraphrases the verse: ". . . . and will make His glory to dwell in the tabernacles of Shem." The final fulfillment of the prediction in Genesis 9:27 came when the Eternal Word, who was with God and was God (John 1:1), was made flesh and tabernacled among us: "and we beheld His glory, the glory as of the only begotten of the Father, full of grace and truth" (John 1:14). He came to His people Israel, who are descendants of Shem, through Abraham (see Gen. 11:10-27).

(3) Later, another choice was made. All of the hundreds of the nations of the world were eliminated except one: the new nation started by God Himself when He called Abraham. So the God of history divides the nations into two groups: Jew and Gentile, and segregates one small nation, the Jews, that through them Messiah might come.

"Now the Lord had said unto Abram . . . get thee out of thy country . . . unto a land that I will show thee . . . and I will make of thee a great nation, and I will bless thee . . . and thou shalt be a blessing . . . and in thee shall all families of the earth be blessed. . . . Unto thy seed will I give this land" (Gen. 12:1-3, 7; see also Gen. 17:1-8, 15-19).

"By Myself have I sworn, saith the Lord . . . that in blessing I will bless thee . . . and in thy seed shall all the nations of the earth be blessed" (Gen. 22:16-18).

Here we have a phenomenon of the first magnitude: a record that goes back 1500 years before Christ **in which the writer hazards multiple predictions:** that God would bless Abraham, make him a blessing, give him the land of Canaan, **and bless the world through him and his "seed."** A great nation was created and given a land of their own for one purpose: that Messiah might come to and through them, to bless the world! The prediction is a literary fact; it has been in the book of Genesis, unchanged, for thousands of years. Its fulfillment is an age-long miracle, and is as definite and complete as the original prophecy. For not only did God make of Abraham a great nation, giving Canaan to the Jews under the conquest of Joshua, but in due time Messiah came to them, and the world has been immeasurably blessed through Abraham's Seed, which is Christ (see Galatians 3:8, 16).

"And the scripture, foreseeing that God would justify the Gentiles through faith, preached before the gospel unto Abraham, saying, In thee shall all nations be blessed."

"Now to Abraham and his seed were the promises made. He saith not, and to seeds, as of many, but as of one, and to thy seed, which is Christ" (Gal. 3:8, 16).

"The book of the generation of Jesus Christ, the son of David, THE SON OF ABRAHAM" (Matt. 1:1).

So the Messianic story slowly unfolds in the Old Testament: Messiah must be the "Seed of the woman," come through the line of Shem, and be "the Seed of Abraham." That narrows our search for Messiah: we now know we must look for Him in the Jewish race, as a descendant of Abraham.

(4) But Abraham had several sons, including Ishmael his firstborn, and Isaac. So, another choice had to be made. We are now informed that Messiah was to come through Isaac (Gen. 17:19; 21:12; cf. Heb. 11:18; Rom. 9:7—"in Issac shall thy seed by called"), and not through Ishmael, the progenitor of the modern Arabs. That narrows the line still more.

"And the Lord appeared unto him (Isaac), and said . . . unto thee, and unto thy seed, I will give all these countries (the promised land), and I will perform the oath which I sware unto Abraham thy father; and I will make thy seed to multiply as the stars of heaven . . . and in thy seed shall all the nations of the earth be blessed" (Gen. 26:2-4).

That Messiah and the promised blessing must come through Isaac and the Jewish race, not the Arabs, is further emphasized in Deuteronomy 18:18, where it is distinctly stated that Messiah, the Great Prophet yet to come, will be raised up "from the midst of thee" (i.e., Israel), "of thy brethren."

This fact is also clearly given in the New Testament:

"Who are Israelites . . . whose are the fathers, and of whom as concerning the flesh Christ came, who is over all, God, blessed for ever"
(Rom. 9:5).

(5) Since Isaac had two sons, the Messianic line must be
further narrowed. The prediction is clearly made that Christ
must come through **Jacob,** not Esau; that is, Messiah could
not be an Edomite (the descendants of Esau).

"And behold the Lord . . . said, I am the Lord God of Abraham thy
father, and the God of Isaac: the land whereon thou liest, to thee will I
give it, and to thy seed . . . and in thy seed shall all families of the earth
be blessed" (Gen. 28:13, 14).

"I shall see Him, but not now: I shall behold Him, but not nigh: there
shall come a Star out of Jacob, and a Sceptre shall rise out of Israel . . .
Out of Jacob shall come He that shall have dominion" (Numb. 24:17, 19).

(6) But Jacob had **twelve** sons: so another choice had to be
made by the Almighty. One of the twelve, JUDAH, is selected.
So, Messiah can not come from eleven of the twelve tribes of
Israel, He must come through **Judah.** (See Genesis 49:8-12).

"Moreover, he refused the tabernacle of Joseph, and chose not the tribe
of Ephraim; but **chose the tribe of Judah**" (Ps. 78:67-68).

"For Judah prevailed above his brethren and of him is (to come) the
chief ruler" (Heb. of 1 Chron. 5:2). Note—the word ruler in the original
is **Nagid,** the same word as in Daniel 9:25, where it is applied to Messiah.

"The sceptre shall not depart from JUDAH, nor a lawgiver from between his feet, until SHILOH come; and unto Him shall the gathering of
the people be" (Gen. 49:10).

Coming to the New Testament, we read that Jesus our
Lord **"sprang out of Judah"** (see Hebrews 7:14; Rev. 5:5).

(7) Next, of the thousands of families in the tribe of Judah,
another choice must be made: Messiah must come from ONE
family line, from the family of **Jesse,** the father of David.

"There shall come forth a rod out of the stem of Jesse, and a Branch
shall grow out of his roots; and the Spirit of the Lord shall rest upon
HIM . . ." (Isa. 11:1-2).

The word "rod" appears in but one other passage in the
Old Testament (Prov. 14:3), and carries the meaning of "a
twig, a shoot such as starts up from the roots of a cut down
tree stump." The passage in Isaiah 11:1-2 is a clear statement that God will take a man with no standing—a mere
"stump" of a tree cut down—and ingraft new life into it.
Jesse was not the head of a royal family, until God made him

the father of a king (David), and put him into the Messianic line!

(8) Since Jesse had eight sons, another Divine choice must be made: Messiah is to be a descendant of DAVID, Jesse's youngest son.

"I will set up thy seed after thee, which shall proceed out of thy bowels, and I will establish his kingdom. He shall build an house for my name, and I will establish the throne of his kingdom for ever"* (2 Sam. 7:12,13). See also 1 Chron. 7:11, 14; Ps. 89:35-37; Jerem. 23:5-6.

"The Lord hath sworn in truth unto David; He will not turn from it; of the fruit of thy body will I set upon thy throne" (Ps. 132:11).

From this last passage quoted (Ps. 132:11) we see that the Lord not only made a promise to David, He confirmed His promise by an oath. God had done the same for Abraham (see Heb. 6:13-18).

Turning to the New Testament, we read:

"The book of the generation of Jesus Christ, THE SON OF DAVID, . . ." (Matt. 1:1).

"Concerning His Son Jesus Christ our Lord, which . . . was made of the seed of David according to the flesh" (Rom. 1:3; cf. 2 Tim. 2:7, 8; Rev. 5:5, 6; 22:16; Acts 2:30-32; Luke 1:30-35).

"And when Jesus departed thence, two blind men followed Him, crying and saying, Thou son of David, have mercy on us" (Matt. 9:27).

"A woman of Capernaum . . . cried unto Him, saying, Have mercy on me, O Lord, thou son of David" (Matt. 15:22).

The public knew Jesus as "the Son of David" and so called Him. (See Matthew 9:27; 12:22-23; 15:22; 20:30,31; 21:9, 15; Mark 9:10: 10:47-48: Luke 18:38-39).

The Pharisees knew full well that Messiah must be the Son of David. When Jesus asked them, "What think ye of Christ (Messiah)? whose son is he?" they answered, "The son of David" (see Matt. 22:41-46).

---

*Mark Lev in his book "Lectures on Messianic Prophecy" (p. 125) comments on the next verse (2 Sam. 7:14), which reads in the AV, "I will be his father, and he shall be my son. If he commit iniquity, I will chasen him with the rod of men, and with the stripes of the children of men." Mr. Lev says, "This could be rendered 'For iniquity committed (not by Him, but my men) I will chasten Him with the rod due to men, and with the stripes due to the children of men.' " This speaks of vicarious sufferings of the Son of David, and agrees with Isaiah 53:6. If the AV rendering be correct, it is a reference of the backslidings and consequent chastening of Solomon, David's immediate successor.

It is obvious Messiah had to be a son of David, according to the flesh—and Jesus was.

The Genealogical Records

During Bible times, every Jew could trace his genealogy. "So all Israel were reckoned by genealogies" (1 Chron. 9:1). These records were kept in the cities (Neh. 7:5, 6; Ezra 2:1) and were public property. Each Israelite's genealogical record constituted his title to his farm or home—so he had a pecuniary interest in preserving the genealogical records of his family. These national genealogical records were carefully kept **until the destruction of Jerusalm and the temple and the Jewish state** in 70 A. D. During the life of Jesus, no one offered to dispute the well known fact that He was of the house and lineage of David, because it was in the public records that all had access to.

Since 70 A.D., when Israel's genealogical records, except those in the Bible, were destroyed or confused, **no pretending Messiah can prove he is the son of David as prophecy demands.** In other words, Messiah **had** to come before 70 A. D.

(9) Moreover, of all David's "many sons," Messiah must get His right to the throne of David through **Solomon's** regal line.

"And of all my sons (for the Lord hath given me many sons), **He hath chosen Solomon my son** to sit upon the throne of the kingdom of the Lord over Israel" (1 Chron. 28:5; cf. v. 6; also, 1 Chron. 29:24).

In the New Testament, Solomon is in the royal line from David to Joseph (see Matthew 1:6).

(10) Yet another most important "specification" about Messiah's lineage is given: **He must be born of a virgin.** And since Messiah must be of the fruit of David's body (Ps. 132:11) **this virgin must be a direct descendant of king David.**

"Hear ye now, O house of David . . . the Lord Himself shall give you a sign (a 'sign' in the Bible is a 'wonder' a 'miracle'); Behold, a virgin*

---

*The new Revised Standard Version of the Bible is grossly in error in translating the Hebrew word **almah** in Isaiah 7:14 as "young woman." Almah refers to a virgin in every instance of its use in the Old Testament (one of which is Exodus 2:8, where it is used of a maid, a young girl, the baby Moses' sister). In the Septuagint **almah** is translated by **parthenos,** the Greek word for virgin.

shall conceive, and bear a son, and shall call his name Immanuel (God with us)" (Isa. 7:13, 14).

It is remarkable that whenever the birth of the Messiah is spoken of in the Old Testament, reference is made to His mother—or the womb—never to a human father. See:

Isaiah 49:1: "The Lord hath called me from the womb".
Isaiah 49:5: "And now saith the Lord that formed me from the womb to be His servant".
Jeremiah 31:22: "The Lord hath created a new thing in the earth: A woman shall encompass a man."
Psalm 22:9: "Thou art he that took me out of the womb."
Micah 5:3: ". . . until the time that she who travaileth hath brought forth."

Turning to the New Testament we find that Jesus indeed was born of a virgin, a virgin who was a direct descendant of King David. After listing the genealogical record from Abraham to Christ, using the oft-repeated phrase as "Abraham begat Isaac, Isaac begat Jacob," etc., showing descent by natural generation, we finally come to the striking statement:

"Now the birth of Jesus Christ was on THIS wise: when as his mother Mary was espoused to Joseph, before they came together, she was found with child of the Holy Spirit . . . for that which is conceived in her is of the Holy Spirit. And she shall bring forth a son, and thou shalt call his name JESUS: for he shall save his people from their sins. Now all this was done that it might be fulfilled which was spoken of the Lord by the prophet, saying, Behold, a virgin shall be with child, and shall bring forth a son, and they shall call his name Emmanuel, which being interpreted is, God with us" (Matt. 1:18, 20-23).

We are dependent on a good woman, Mary, a good man, Joseph, a good doctor, Luke, a faithful recorder, Matthew, the word of an angel, and the word of God who gave both the prediction and its literal fulfillment, for an honest, accurate account of the birth of Jesus. See Matthew 1:16-23; Luke 1:28-35; Luke 2:1-20.

Here indeed is a sign—a WONDER—that only God can fulfill. Obviously, no Messianic pretender can cause himself to be born of a virgin. And since "every truth is consistent with every other truth in the universe" it would not only be difficult, it would be impossible for a pretender to collect five such good witnesses as Mary, Joseph, Luke, Matthew and the angel of the Lord to lie for him without the fraud being detected sooner or later.* We can depend on the testimony of these five witnesses.

This much is clear: who ever the Almighty sent to earth via the virgin birth is the Messiah: for here is a true "sign," a wonder of heavenly origin, that cannot be faked. The God who gave the specification in Isaiah 7:14 fulfilled it in the virgin birth of Jesus. We see the truth of Jeremiah 1:12RV: "Jehovah said . . . I watch over My word to perform it."

Remember, this Messianic chain giving Messiah's lineage was formed through many centuries: from Eve, to David, to Isaiah, to the prophet Micah's time. It was added to by many human agents, who spoke "in diverse manners, times and places." And every time Prophecy made a particular choice, there was a new risk, humanly speaking, of selecting the wrong branch, and nothing short of **absolute accuracy** will do when God claims to speak.**

"Absolute accuracy" it was: for when Messiah came He fulfilled to the letter ALL the specifications of His lineage and was indeed "the Seed of the woman," "the Son of Abraham, the Son of David" (Matt. 1:1). No other person in all the world than Jesus of Nazareth could meet all, or even a small part, of these specifications.

Let us illustrate. Remember, there are no two people exactly alike in all the world—not even identical twins. Suppose you are "George Bardon." You live at 113 Smith Drive, Detroit, Mich. You are five feet ten inches tall; you weigh 165 pounds. You are married and have five children: three boys and two girls. You sell life insurance for a living. You have $5,124.76 in the bank. Manifestly **no one else in all the world has ALL of your "specifications."** It is easy to see, if enough characteristic details are given, identification is positive; the same is true of prophecy: if a sufficient number of details are given, **identification is positive.** So many details of

---

*A literary fraud is well-nigh impossible, for each lie exposes itself sooner or later by NOT being "consistent with other known truths in the universe." Scholars, by knowing contemporary history, geography, philology and the manners and customs of the era can easily detect a literary fraud, for it will not fit in with the known facts in those realms.

**A. T. Pierson, in God's Living Oracles.

Messiah are given, and each one is exactly fulfilled in Jesus of Nazareth, so identification is positive.

(11) To further help all know Messiah when He came, **the Place of His birth is given.** Prophecy has given us His "address" in terms of the town where He was to be born.

"But thou, BETHLEHEM Ephratah, though thou be little among the thousands of Judah, yet out of thee shall he come forth unto me that is to be ruler in Israel; whose goings forth have been from of old, from everlasting" (Mic. 5:2).

Of all the continents, one is chosen: Asia; of all states, one is chosen: Canaan. All provinces of Palestine are eliminated save one: Judea; all cities of Judea are eliminated save one: Bethlehem Ephratah—a tiny village having at that time fewer than a thousand inhabitants. The prophet pin-points one obscure village on the map of the world, but he speaks infallibly, for the omniscient God was behind his utterance. The prophet spoke clearly, too, with unequivocal certainty; for when King Herod demanded of the chief priests and the scribes of the people where Christ should be born, they told him, "In Bethlehem of Judea, for thus it is written by the prophet" (Matt. 2:4-6; cf. John 7:42).

The Drama of Fulfilled Prophecy

Jesus was born in Bethlehem of Judea (Matt. 2:1) in a manner altogether marvelous. Until shortly before the time of Jesus' birth, Mary was living at the wrong place—that is, if her coming baby was the Messiah. Note now the intricacies of God's Providences in fulfilling His Word. In 1923 at Ankara, Turkey, was found a Roman temple inscription (reported by Sir William Ramsay, noted British chemist and archeologist) which, when deciphered, related that in the reign of Caesar Augustus there were three great tax collections. The second was ordered four years before the birth of Christ. The third, several years after His birth. The second one is the one we are concerned with.

The proud Jews resented the idea of a special tax, so they sent a commission to Rome to protest it. Quirinius, the local governor of Syria, had not the authority to settle the problem. Those were days of slow communications and slower travel. The commission finally failed and the Jews had to submit to the enrollment and taxing. But by the time the official tax collectors had worked their way eastward, town by town, and province by province, and after the time-consuming delays caused by the Jewish protests, exactly enough delay was caused, and all in the natural course of events, so that when the enrollment was put in force in Judea **the exact time had come to Mary for the birth of the baby Jesus!**

Neither Mary nor Caesar nor the Roman tax collectors did the timing, nor were they in charge of affairs: but the God who rules the world behind the scenes had His hand on the wheel, and He literally "moved the peoples of the world" and timed everything to the very day, so that Mary and Joseph got to Bethlehem **in the nick of time,** that Jesus, the chosen Messiah, might be born in the right place, the place designated by the infallible finger of prophecy!

Blind indeed is the man who can't see or who won't see the Mind of the Infinite planning these details and the Hand of the Almighty executing His perfect plan!

(12) Finally, to pin-point Messiah, the TIME of His coming, as well as the place, is given. Of all generations of earth's history, Messiah had to come when Jesus was born! All before Jesus' time are eliminated; all after His time are disqualified; and since Jesus of Nazareth had no consequential "competitor" in His generation, the Finger of Prophecy points infallibly to HIM.

There are three general predictions as to the time of Messiah's coming, and one specific.

(A) Messiah must come **before the tribe of Judah lost its tribal identity.**

"The sceptre shall not depart from Judah, nor a lawgiver from between his feet, until Shiloh come; and unto Him shall the obedience of the people be" (Gen. 49:10).

The word "sceptre" in this passage does not necessarily mean a king's staff. The word* translated "sceptre" means primarily a "tribal staff." The **tribal identity** of Judah shall

---

*The word **shebet,** which is translated sceptre in the AV signifies a rod or staff, particularly the rod or staff which belonged to each tribe as an ensign of their authority. Each tribe was in possession of its own peculiar 'rod' or 'staff' with its name inscribed thereon." (Bishop Sherlock's Discourses on Prophecy.) Hence, the "sceptre" signifies their identity as a tribe.

not pass away—as did that of the other ten tribes of Israel—until Shiloh come.

For ages both Jewish and Christian commentators have taken "Shiloh" to be a name of Messiah. It means "Peace" or "One sent."

Even though Judah, during the seventy-year period of their captivity at Babylon, had been deprived of national sovereignty, they **never lost their "tribal staff," their national identity;** and they always had their own "lawgivers" (judges) of their own, even in captivity (Ezra 1:5,8).

At the time of Christ, though the Romans were overlords of the Jews, the Jews had a king in their own land; moreover, they were to large extent governed by their own laws, and the Sanhedrin of the nation still exercised its authority. But in the space of a few years, during the year when Jesus was twelve years of age, when He appeared publicly in the temple (Luke 2:41-52), **Archelaus, the king of the Jews, was dethroned and banished.** Coponius was appointed Roman Procurator, and the kingdom of Judah, the last remnant of the former greatness of the nation Israel, was formally debased into a part of the province of Syria.* For almost another half century the Jews retained the semblance of a provincial governmental structure; but in 70 A.D. both their city and their temple were destroyed by the armies of the Roman General Titus, and all semblance of Jewish national sovereignty disappeared. But the remarkable thing is this: Messiah (Shiloh) came **before** Judah lost its tribal identity, exactly as stated in Genesis 49:10!

(B) Messiah must come **while the second temple was still standing.**

---

*See Josephus' Antiquities 17, Chapter 13:1-5.

Twenty-two years before the Lord Jesus was crucified, the Sanhedrin lost the power of passing the death sentence (see John 18:31) when Judea became a Roman province, as mentioned above. Rabbi Rachmon says, "When the members of the Sanhedrin found themselves deprived of their right over life and death, a general consternation took possession of them; they covered their heads with ashes and their bodies with sackcloth, exclaiming, "Woe unto us, for the sceptre has departed from Judah and the Messiah has not come'." (Chosen People). The rabbis did not realize that Messiah **had** come. From this it is apparent that they considered Genesis 49:10 Messianic, and had a clear concept of its meaning.

"And I will shake all nations, and the desire of all nations shall come: and I will fill this house with glory, saith the Lord of hosts. . . . The glory of this latter house shall be greater than of the former, saith the Lord of hosts: and in this place will I give peace, saith the Lord of hosts" (Hag. 2:7-9).

Malachi confirms the prediction in Haggai 2:7-9; "the Lord shall suddenly **come to His temple.**" This prediction in Malachi, as well as the one in Haggai, could **not** be fulfilled **after** the destruction of the temple in 70 A.D. So, if Messiah came at all, He had to come before the temple was destroyed. Zechariah 11:13 also demands that Messiah come before the destruction of the Jewish temple, for that prediction speaks of "the thirty pieces of silver" being "cast to the potter **in the House of the Lord**" (the temple) (Zech. 11:13). In Psalm 118:26 the prophetic pen informs us that the people who should welcome Messiah would say not only "Blessed be He that cometh in the name of the Lord" but also "We have blessed you **out of the house of the Lord**" (Ps. 118:26). That is, from the House of the Lord (the temple) the people will bless Him when He comes.

This was beautifully fulfilled in the life of Jesus. When He approached Jerusalem, for His triumphal entry, the people said, "Blessed is He that cometh in the name of the Lord; Hosanna in the highest" (Matt. 21:9). Then we read that Jesus healed many that were blind and lame **in the temple** (Matt. 21:14), and there can be no doubt that those who were healed in the temple "blessed Him in the House of the Lord," even as Psalm 118:26 said they would! And there is another definite fulfillment to the prediction: Matthew 21:15 tells us that the children cried **in the temple,** saying, "Hosanna to the son of David." Surely, "out of the mouth of babes and sucklings Thou hast perfected praise" (Ps. 8:2; Matt. 21:16)—and God used **children** to fulfill His prediction given in Psalm 118:26 that Messiah should be blessed in the House of the Lord!

There are at least five Scriptural predictions of the coming of Messiah **that demand that He come while the temple at Jerusalem was still standing.** This is a fact of great significance, since the temple has NOT been rebuilt since its destruction in 70 A.D. These five Scriptures are: Haggai 2:7-9; Malachi 3:1; Zechariah 11:13; Daniel 9:26 and Psalm 118:26.

Therefore, the public entry of Jesus into Jerusalem and into the temple as recorded were all prearranged and predicted and are part of the perfect Plan that foretold Messiah and His activities when He should come, and then perfectly fulfilled the blueprint in the movements of Jesus of Nazareth when He came. See Matthew 21:1-16; Mark 11:1-10; Luke 19:29-40.

"And Jesus went into the temple of God . . . and the blind and the lame came unto Him in the temple; and He healed them . . . and the children crying in the temple, and saying, Hosanna to the son of David;" (Matt. 21:12-15).

Two other intensely interesting Scriptures bear on this; when the child Jesus was taken to the temple by His parents, as recorded in Luke 2:25-32 (please read); also, when Jesus as a boy of twelve was "in the temple, sitting in the midst of the doctors . . . and all that heard Him were astonished at His understanding" (Luke 2:46-47)

After years, yea centuries, of waiting, Messiah suddenly came to His temple! (Mal. 3:1). Then a few years later, God with a dramatic gesture destroyed the temple and the city of Jerusalem, even as Jesus had told the people.* And on the old temple site now stands a heathen shrine, the Mosque of Omar. Providence, by these significant facts, is saying to all Jews, to all people everywhere, Messiah has already come! He can't come now, there is no temple. Messiah had to come 1900 years ago, before I had the temple destroyed.

Either Jesus of Nazareth is the true Messiah, or there is no Messiah, no prophecy, no Word of God, no God, no objective truth; and then all history, as well as all the future, is as meaningless as the babbling of a dribbling idiot and as purposeless as the driftwood on the outskirts of a maddening whirlpool.

(C) Daniel says something remarkable about the coming of

---

*Jesus told them that the temple, the heart of their worship, yea the heart and soul of their very national existence, would be torn down, and "not one stone left upon another" (Matt. 24:2). As Jesus the true Prophet had said, so it came to pass—no doubt sooner than the disciples expected.

Christ relative to the temple. In giving the time-table from his time to the coming of Messiah (see the next paragraph) Daniel makes it very clear that Messiah will come and be "cut off" (die) **before** the "people (the Romans) of the prince that shall come shall destroy the city (Jerusalem) and the sanctuary" (the temple) (Dan. 9:26). Since we have already discussed this under point "B" (above) we pass on to our next fact relative to the time of Messiah's coming.

(D) Messiah must come **483 years after a specific date in Daniel's time.** This definite prediction as to the exact TIME of the coming of Messiah is one of the most wonderful prophecies in the entire Bible. It establishes the date of Messiah's advent almost five hundred years before He came. Here is the prediction:

"Know therefore and understand, that from the going forth of the commandment to restore and to build Jerusalem unto MESSIAH THE PRINCE shall be seven weeks, and threescore and two weeks: the streets shall be built again, and the wall, even in troublous times. And after threescore and two weeks shall Messiah be cut off, but not for Himself: and the people of the prince that shall come shall destroy the city and the sanctuary" (Dan. 9:25, 26).

The date of the "commandment to restore and to build Jerusalem" was the decree by Artaxerxes in 444 B.C.* granting permission to the Jews to return to Palestine and rebuild the city of Jerusalem (see Nehemiah 2:1-8).

The Hebrew word translated "weeks" in the Scripture quoted above (Dan. 9:25,26) means "sevens" or heptads, and is used for years. (See Lev. 25:8; Gen. 29:27-28). In other words, the "seventy sevens" that are prophetically determined on Israel and on the holy city, with specified events (v. 24), **is a period of 490 years.** This period is divided into three sections: (1) Seven "weeks," or seven sevens of years—the 49 years the prophet allotted for the rebuilding of Jerusalem under the leadership of Nehemiah and Ezra and those associated

---

*Some authorities differ as to the exact date, the dates given ranging from 454 to 444 B.C., within a ten-year period. In any event, the 483 years that begin with this event bring us to the time of Jesus of Nazareth. For a detailed discussion of this amazing prediction, see Sir Robert Anderson's book "The Coming Prince"; also see John Urquhart's "Wonders of Prophecy" and Mark Lev's "Lectures on Messianic Prophecy."

with them (see the books of Nehemiah and Ezra). History tells us it took 49 years to do this rebuilding job. (2) A second period of 62 "weeks," or 434 years, which would bring the time to MESSIAH. (3) The 70th "week," a period of seven years some time after the coming of Messiah.

We now are especially interested in the period "from the commandment to restore and to build Jerusalem" to "Messiah the Prince," which totals to a period of 483 years. Sir Robert Anderson in his book "The Coming Prince," figured it out, and gave the world his findings. We quote from the facts he presents:

He starts with March 14, 444 B. C., the date of the commandment to restore and build Jerusalem; and he ends the period with Jesus' triumphal entry into Jerusalem (which he believes was the official presentation of Messiah as "Prince" to Israel. Cf. Luke 19:38-40 with Zech. 9:9). After careful investigation and consultation with noted astronomers, he gives these startling findings: From 444 B. C. to 32 A. D. is 476 years; 476 x 365 is 173,740 days; from March 14 to April 6 (the day of Christ's triumphal entry) is 24 days; add 116 days for leap years, and you get a total of 173,880 days. Since the "prophetic year" of the Bible is always 360 days, the 69 "sevens" of this prophecy in Daniel (69 x 7 x 360) is 173,880 days! And so the time given by Daniel from the "commandment to restore and build Jerusalem" to "Messiah the Prince" comes out perfectly—to the very day!

This is a genuine prophecy, as detailed as a road map, with no taint of ambiguity: and it is a prediction that can be proven true. It is a sign that points unerringly to JESUS OF NAZARETH who was "Messiah the Prince," who was "cut off" (by a violent death) but not for Himself. When Jesus began His public ministry, He said significantly, "The TIME is fulfilled and the kingdom of God is at hand" (Mark 1:15). Messiah must be born at some time; it might have been in any century, in any year; but with absolute certainty the exact year, the very month of a notable event in His life, is foretold.

We now have given twelve points, showing Messiah's Credentials. These were given in the Prophetic Word so that all might know Messiah when He came. The accuracy of prediction is minute; the fulfillment is exact. One mistake would be fatal—but all is in perfect agreement: Jesus of Nazareth fulfills ALL the specifications as to His lineage, His birthplace, and the time of His birth. And is it not most remarkable that within a generation of Christ's sufferings on the cross the temple was destroyed, the Jewish priesthood ceased to exist, the sacrifices were no longer offered, the Jews' genealogical records were destroyed, their city was destroyed, and the people of Israel were driven out of their land, sold into slavery, and dispersed to the four corners of the earth! Since those dreadful national judgments fell on Israel it has been utterly impossible for a "Messiah" to come with proper "credentials," such as the Old Testament demands, and such as Jesus of Nazareth presented.

II. PROPHECIES CONCERNING THE LIFE AND MINISTRY OF MESSIAH

(1) **Messiah's Character and Characteristics are clearly Delineated: He will be the Sinless One—as holy as God.***

Messiah must be as righteous as the Lord Himself: for He will be the "righteous Branch . . . who shall be called THE LORD OUR RIGHTEOUSNESS" (Jerem. 23:5,6). Messiah must be God's chosen One in whom He will "delight" (Isa. 42:1). In Matthew 3:17 we read that the Father said of Jesus, "This is my beloved Son, in whom I am well pleased." Messiah, on His part, will be the obedient "Servant of the Lord" who will ever "delight to do God's will" (Ps. 40:8). The Lord Jesus could testify, "My meat is to do the will of Him that sent Me, and to finish His work" (John 4:34; see also John 6:38).

Messiah will be anointed by the Holy Spirit in a manner and degree far beyond any man or men ("above" His fellows, Ps. 45:7; cf. Heb. 1:9). Read the remarkable passage in Isaiah 11:3-6 that tells us:

"And the Spirit of the Lord shall rest upon Him, the spirit of wisdom and understanding, the spirit of counsel and might, the spirit of knowledge and of the fear of the Lord; and shall make Him of quick understanding in the fear of the Lord: and He shall not judge after the sight of His eyes, neither reprove after the hearing of His ears: but with righteousness shall He judge the poor. . . . And righteousness shall be the girdle of His loins, and faithfulness the girdle of His reins" (Isa. 11:2-5).

* For a delightful Bible reading, look up these Scriptures on the character of Messiah: Ps. 40:6-10; Ps. 45:1-8; Isa. 11:2-5; Isa. 42:1-7; Isa. 63:1-3; Isa. 53:7-9.

In the New Testament, we read of Jesus' anointing with the Holy Spirit at the time of His baptism, when the Holy Spirit like a dove descended and lit upon Him (Matt. 3:16). He bare witness that the "Spirit of the Lord" was upon Him (Luke 4:18), which was in fulfillment of a prediction about Messiah's character and ministry in Isaiah 61:1-3. The people "bare Him (Jesus) witness, and wondered at the gracious words that proceeded out of His mouth" (Luke 4:22).

Messiah must be a man of perfect self-control: "His voice (in anger, or as an excited rabble-rouser) shall not be heard in the streets" (Isa. 42:2); He will have patience with the frailties of men: "He shall not break the bruised reed, nor quench the smoking flax" (Isa. 42:3); Messiah will have perseverance in the course of doing right, His Father's will; He will have courage and success in that goal, as well as steadfastness of purpose: "He shall neither fail nor be discouraged" (Isa. 42:4). Matthew, in describing the ministry of Jesus, says that Jesus fulfilled what Isaiah had said about Him:

"That it might be fulfilled which was spoken by Isaiah the prophet, saying, Behold My Servant, whom I have chosen; My Beloved, in whom My soul is well pleased; I will put My Spirit upon Him, and He shall show judgment to the Gentiles. He shall not strive, nor cry; neither shall any man hear His voice in the streets. A bruised reed shall He not break, and smoking flax shall He not quench, till He send forth judgment unto victory. And in His name shall the Gentiles trust" (Matt. 12:17-21).

Messiah's compassion and tenderness are revealed in an exquisite figure of touching tenderness: "He shall gather the lambs with His arms, and carry them in His bosom, and shall gently lead those that are with young" (Isa. 40:11). "He shall feed His flock like a shepherd" (Isa. 40:11f.c.). In the New Testament we read of the compassion of Jesus in Matthew 9:36; 14:14; 15:32, and many other places. In the tenth chapter of John, Christ is presented as the "Good Shepherd" who loves His sheep and cares for them, even giving His life for them (John 10:10-18).

Messiah will be "just and lowly" (Zech. 9:9), "fairer than the children of men" with "grace poured into His lips" and blessed by God for ever (Ps. 45:2). He will be "without violence"—a blameless outward life—"and without deceit"—an innocent inner life (Isa. 53:9; cf. 1 Pet. 2:22). He will suffer great personal wrong done to Him without complaining either to God or man (Isa. 53:7; Isa. 50:4,6,7). Coming to the New Testament, we learn that Jesus "is meek and lowly in heart" (Matt. 11:29); and the Father testified of Him, "Thou hast loved righteousness and hated iniquity; therefore God . . . hath anointed Thee with the oil of gladness above Thy fellows" (Heb. 1:9). When the Lord Jesus was crucified, He meekly suffered all the indignities, the insults, the blasphemies, the mental torture, the physical violence heaped upon Him, and did not complain; in fact, He prayed for His persecutors (Luke 23:34; Matt. 27:12-14).

As a teacher, Messiah "shall not fail . . . till He have set judgment* in the earth" and the nations "shall wait on His teaching" (Isa. 42:4). Today, multitudes in our most advanced nations "wait on Jesus' teaching" and when finally the kingdom of God, with Christ as king, is set up on earth, He will indeed have "set judgment in the earth."

It was prewritten of Messiah that He would "open His mouth with parables" . . . He will "utter things hidden from the foundation of the world" (Ps. 78:2). When Jesus the Great Teacher came, He taught "as one having authority, and not as the scribes" (Matt. 7:29). The scribes taught by quoting what such-and-such a Rabbi had said; but when Jesus taught, He gave God's words and spoke with finality and assurance: "Verily, verily, I say unto you . . ." (see John 5:24; 6:47, etc.). Moreover, Christ's characteristic method of teaching was by the use of parables—"for without a parable spake He nothing unto them: **that it might be fulfilled which was spoken through the prophet, saying, I will open my mouth in parables**" (Matt. 13:34,35).

It is plain from the reading of the Old Testament that when Messiah comes, He will be holier and wiser than men, even as just and righteous as God himself. Who in all the history of the world could this be speaking of, other than Jesus the Christ, who was "holy, harmless, undefiled, separate

---

*The word translated "judgment" is a very rich word, translated by 31 different words in the AV. It means to bring justice, law, order, salvation, truth, righteousness, to mankind. Messiah's ministry was to bring Salvation and Truth ("judgment") to Gentiles as well as to Jews (Isa. 42:6).

from sinners, and made higher than the heavens" (Heb. 7:26).

The Miracle of All Literature: the Portrayal of the Perfect Character

Now we come to the miracle of all literature: the portrayal of the Perfect Character, Jesus the Christ in the New Testament. That which is given in general terms, in an abstract way, in the Old Testament, in the portrayal of the coming perfect Messiah, becomes a concrete reality, in the flesh, in the Person of Jesus the Christ in the New Testament. In the Lord Jesus we see the One who is altogether lovely, the chiefest among ten thousand, the delight of the Heavenly Father.*

Christ's perfectly poised character was not unbalanced by eccentricities or human foibles. His perfections were not tainted by pride, nor was His wisdom marred by an occasional bit of folly. His equity was not twisted by prejudice, nor was His justice adulterated by selfish whims. He had a becoming dignity that was happily blended with His gracious humility. He had concern for others without worry, zeal without fretfulness, patience without dilatoriness, tact without dishonesty, and frankness without rudeness. His authority was balanced and blended with gentleness and patience.

He never had to admit defeat, retract a statement, offer an apology, change His teachings, confess a sin or a mistake, or ask advice. He never lost His temper, or spoke rashly. He was never bested in an argument: He always had the right answer —the will and the word of God.

He went about doing good, prayed much, gave God the glory and thanks in all things, had no interest in the accumulation of material things; He lived and died in poverty—yet He never lacked until His sufferings on the cross.

His miracles were all beneficent—never for vainglory. He was the perfect Teacher who lived what He taught. He was one of us in the truest sense: "the Son of man"; yet He was not one of us, for He never sinned. He was from Above and

---

* Contrast with Christ the wily Mohammed who pretended to receive a divine warrant to sanction his past impurities and to license his future crimes. How different was the Lord Jesus! He said, "If I do not the works of My Father, believe Me not" (John 10:37).

not from the earth, and He was the unique Son of God. Never man spake like this man.

He never made a claim to supernatural power or prerogative but what He performed a miracle of like kind to prove it. He who said "I am the Light of the world" (John 9:5) also opened the eyes of the man born blind, so all could see His right to the claim. He who said "I am the resurrection and the life" (John 11:25-27) proved that these were sober words of truth by raising Lazarus from the dead! (John 11:25,43,44). He who said "I am the bread of life" (John 6:35) gave full evidence that He was all He claimed to be by performing the miracle of feeding the five thousand from a few loaves and fewer fish (John 6:5-14). If Jesus were not the true Messiah, the Saviour of the world, what an unmitigated crime against humanity, what brash folly, what unforgivable egotism, for Him to make the promises He did, and so deceive people for time and eternity. Certainly such evil could not come from One as good and as loving as Jesus. We believe and are sure that He is indeed the Christ, the Son of God, the One who should come into the world to be the Redeemer of mankind.

Volumes have been written, volumes more will be written, on the moral glory, the perfect character of the Lord Jesus. Suffice it to say in summary: He is the image of the invisible God (Heb. 1:3), the sum and substance of all good, the One in whom dwelt all the fulness of the Godhead (Col. 2:9). His holiness shone with undimmed lustre; His loveliness was as pure and genuine as the glory of God. His love was as selfless and as complete as the love of God—for in all the history of the world mankind has never seen, except in the death of Christ, "a perfect character dying under an unparalleled weight of unmerited agony." The mighty yet lowly Royal Sufferer uncomplainingly bore the weight of the sin of the race in His atoning death on the cross.

(2) **Messiah's Supernatural "Miracle" Works are clearly Foretold: He must show as His Hallmarks Supernatural Works that show Him to be the God-appointed, God-sent Redeemer. And as His "Special" Work, Messiah will offer Himself as a Substitutionary Sacrifice to redeem the Race.**

Messiah's whole ministry must BLESS the people. As Isaiah foretold:

"The Spirit of the Lord God is upon Me; because the Lord hath anointed Me to preach good tidings unto the meek; He hath sent Me to bind up the broken-hearted, to proclaim liberty to the captives, and the opening of the prison to them that are bound; to proclaim the acceptable year of the Lord . . . to give unto them beauty for ashes, the oil of joy for mourning, the garment of praise for the spirit of heaviness" (Isa. 61:1-3).

Messiah, as the Lord God in the midst of the people, must be the miracle worker par excellence:

"Behold your God will come . . . He will come and save you. Then the eyes of the blind shall be opened, and the ears of the deaf shall be unstopped. Then shall the lame man leap as a hart, and the tongue of the dumb sing" (Isa. 35:4-6).

"I the Lord have called thee in righteousness . . . and give thee for a covenant of the people, and for a light of the Gentiles; to open the blind eyes, to bring out the prisoners from the prison . . ." (Isa. 42:6,7).

Messiah will be the worldwide SAVIOUR for "salvation to the ends of the earth" (Isa. 49:6): as a "Light to the Gentiles" (Isa. 42:6-7; Isa. 11:10), and the "Redeemer of Israel" (Isa. 49:7; also. Isa. 42:6).

In the New Testament, Christ is the worldwide Saviour:

"For God so loved the WORLD that He gave His only begotten Son, that whosoever believeth in Him should not perish, but have everlasting life" (John 3:16).

The prophet Simeon, in the temple, when he saw the child Jesus, knew this was the Christ. He said, "Lord, . . . mine eyes have seen Thy salvation, which Thou hast prepared before the face of all people; a Light to lighten the Gentiles, and the Glory of Thy people Israel" (Luke 2:29-32). See also Luke 1:68-79; Rom. 3:28-30, etc.

Messiah's **special** work will be to offer Himself, His soul and body, as a ransom, an offering, a sacrifice, for sin and sinners (see Isaiah 53:4-6,10,12). By this supreme sacrifice of Himself, He will "bruise Satan's head" (Gen. 3:15 with Heb. 2:14; 1 John 3:8); and by that great work of redemption He will establish a kingdom that will last for ever (Dan. 7:14; Isa. 9:7; Luke 1:32-33; Heb. 2:9-14).

Turning to the New Testament again, we see the identification of the Old Testament Messiah with the Christ of the New to be perfect, as far as His holy character, His "works" and His special "work" on the cross are concerned.

The miracles that Jesus wrought—His works—**were well**

known by His generation. Peter in his sermon on the day of Pentecost uses the fact of Christ's miracle-working ministry as PROOF of His Messiahship.

"Ye men of Israel, hear these words; Jesus of Nazareth, a man approved of God among you by MIRACLES and WONDERS and SIGNS, which God did by Him in the midst of you, **as ye yourselves also know** . . . Therefore let all the house of Israel know assuredly, that God hath made that same Jesus, whom ye have crucified (whom God hath raised up) both LORD AND CHRIST" (Acts 2:22,36,24).

In the Gospels we read that Jesus blessed, saved and helped all seekers who contacted Him: He healed the sick, cleansed the lepers, opened the eyes of the blind, raised the dead, fed the hungry, walked on the Sea of Galilee, and performed many other miracles.*

John the Baptist, after his imprisonment by king Herod, sent two of his disciples to Jesus to ask Him, "Art thou He that should come (the Messiah), or do we look for another?" (Matt. 11:2-3), thereby putting a direct question to Jesus: "Are you Messiah or are you not?" Jesus answered by reminding John and his disciples of His MIRACLE WORKS, thus assuring them He was Messiah for **Messiah alone could do those works:**

"Go and show John again those things which ye do hear and see: The blind receive their sight, and the lame walk, the lepers are cleansed, the deaf hear, the dead are raised up, and the poor have the Gospel preached to them" (Matt. 11:4-5)—and THESE THINGS ARE THE VERY MARKS OF MESSIAH GIVEN IN THE OLD TESTAMENT!

Finally, after His benevolent ministry of healing and blessing the people, Christ accomplished the great work for which He came into the world, to which work He was foreordained from before the foundation of the world (see 1 Pet. 1:18-20); He died on the cross, offering Himself as a vicarious sacrifice to redeem the race.

"Christ Jesus, who gave Himself a ransom for all" (1 Tim. 2:6).

"Jesus . . . by the grace of God . . . tasted death for every man" (Heb. 2:9).

"Christ . . . once in the end of the ages appeared to put away sin by the sacrifice of Himself" (Heb. 9:26).

---

* See Mark 1:32,34,41,42; John 9:7; John 11:43,44; John 6:11-13; John 6:19-21, etc., etc.

Jesus Himself appealed to the people to believe on Him for "the very works' sake" (John 14:10-11).

"Believest thou not that I am in the Father, and the Father in Me? the words that I speak unto you I speak not of Myself: but the Father that dwelleth in Me, He doeth the works. Believe Me that I am in the Father, and the Father in Me: or else believe Me for the very works' sake" (John 14:10-11).

No mere pretender can have this TRIPLE SEAL as proof of his genuineness: (1) Have a perfect character; (2) perform "miracle" works; (3) offer Himself as a Sacrifice for the redemption of the race. These three requirements not only eliminate all fake "Messiahs," but also clearly establish the fact that Jesus of Nazareth is the true Messiah, for He fulfilled all three!

During the last nineteen centuries His gospel has literally been preached around the world, and millions upon millions of Gentiles as well as multitudes of Jews, have trusted and are trusting Him. Jesus is indeed the universal Saviour, the "Lamb of God who taketh away the sin of the world" (John 1:29). His love envelopes the world (John 3:16); His gospel is for every creature (Mark 16:15); His is the only Name under Heaven, given among men "whereby we must be saved" (Acts 4:12).

The Overwhelming, cumulative Effect of Added Signs

We have traced the Messianic Line from Shem, through Abraham, Isaac, Jacob, Judah, Jesse, David—and down to the virgin birth, the "Seed of the woman," at the appointed time and place—and we found all perfectly fulfilled in Jesus of of Nazareth, without one failure! We also saw that since all the genealogical records were destroyed in 70 A. D., no Messianic claimant since then can prove his Messiahship.

We have shown that the Old Testament predicts a Messiah with a perfect character, a benevolent ministry characterized by miracles of healing, and that His great work will be to offer Himself as a sacrifice to redeem the people. Jesus of Nazareth, the Christ of the four Gospels, fulfilled all this perfectly. The cumulative effect of one fulfillment after another, without one failure, is staggering.

We present an illustration to show that comparatively few distinctive "signs" are sufficient to identify one individual out of billions.

Identifying David Greenglass

When U. S. authorities got on the trail of the traitor, David Greenglass, who gave atomic secrets to the Russians after World War II, he fled to Mexico. His confederates arranged for him to meet the secretary of the Russian Ambassador in Mexico City, and to identify himself by these prearranged signs. (Identical instructions were given to both Greenglass and the Secretary). (1) He was to write a note to the Secretary and sign his name as "I. Jackson." (2) After three days he was to go to the Plaza de Colon in Mexico City, and (3) stand before the statue of Columbus, (4) with his middle finger placed in a guidebook. (5) When the Secretary approached, Greenglass was to say, it was a magnificent statue; and that he was from Oklahoma. (6) The Secretary then was to give him a passport. Needless to say, the plan worked.*

They knew—all men know—that with as few as six identifying signs, it would be impossible for an impostor to deceive the Secretary, unless he learned what the signs were. God has seen fit to give us not six but scores of signs to identify Messiah and to make the signs of such a nature (such as the virgin birth or resurrection of Messiah) that no false Messiah could possibly fake them! All who take the time **to look into the facts,** such as we are presenting here, **will come to know positively that a Messiah was predicted and that the only One who could be that Messiah is Jesus the Christ of the New Testament.**

We Challenge the World—$1,000 Reward Offered!

We hereby challenge the world with this double challenge; and we will give $1,000 reward to any one proving either of these two propositions:

(1) Show that there is another book than the Bible in the literature of the world that contains prophecies about a coming Messiah, similar to those in the Bible; and after a lapse of

---

* These facts are taken from the April 2, 1951 edition of The New Leader.

four hundred years gives evidence of a definite fulfillment, in twenty or more details.

(2) Produce any "Christ," living or dead (other than Jesus of Nazareth) who can fulfill even half of the predictions concerning Messiah that we give in this book. We would ask of any who claims or who claimed to be the true Messiah:
Was he born in Bethlehem?
Was he born of a virgin?
Is he a direct descendant of both Abraham and David?
Did he come approximately 490 years after Daniel's time?
Did he exercise a benevolent ministry characterized by miracles?
Was he a perfect character?
Did he die on a cross? and rise again the third day?
Did he offer his body to be wounded and pierced, as a sacrifice for the sins of the people?
Did he rise from the dead and ascend to Heaven?
Was he sold for thirty pieces of silver?
Did any ever part his garments or cast lots for his vesture?
Did he ever use the cry, "My God, My God, why hast Thou forsaken Me?"

A moment's thought will convince all fair-minded persons that Jesus the Christ of the New Testament who fulfilled ALL of the 333 prophecies that relate to His first advent is the only character of all history to qualify as the predicted Messiah; and that there is no other book than the Bible that has anything comparable to Messianic predictions, having twenty or more specific details.*

III. PROPHETIC PARADOXES IN PROPHECIES CONCERNING CHRIST

The Old Testament presents a mysterious prophetic puzzle of strange combinations of prophecies concerning the coming Messiah that appear at times so conflicting they seem impossible of fulfillment. We call these prophecies that are seemingly contradictory and apparently irreconcilable **"prophetic paradoxes."** We define a "prophetic paradox" as two or more prophecies that contain a **seeming** contradiction, with no real

* If anyone wishes to lay claim to the $1,000 offered, write out your case, and include a copy of the book which you believe rivals the Bible in its prophecies. This book must, of course, antedate by at least 400 years the destruction of Jerusalem which took place in 70 A.D., for there is no way of proving any Messianic claims after 70 A.D. for all Jewish genealogical records were destroyed at that time.

absurdity involved, and presenting an enigma which, without the "clue" or fulfillment, seems impossible of solution. The Old Testament abounds with such prophetic paradoxes concerning Christ which were and still are absolute mysteries except as the New Testament solves them in Christ. These paradoxes in prophecy have an element of obscurity presenting as it were a LOCK for which only the New Testament has the KEY*—and that key is Jesus the Christ.

This amazing feature of many Messianic predictions prevents both wicked men and over-zealous disciples from purposely fulfilling them—if they could. For the prophecies, in at least some instances, were not fully understood until the fulfillment explained and made them plain. (See I Pet. 1:10, 11). Such unique prophecies absolutely prove that the God of Prophecy who designed them and the God of Providence who fulfilled them are one.

Another astonishing feature about these prophetic paradoxes is the perfectly normal, artless way in which they were providentially, even miraculously, fulfilled in the life of Jesus the Christ in the New Testament. It is not necessary to strain or force either the facts or the predictions to make them match.

Consider for a few moments some of these "impossible" contrasts: God will come to earth—to be born as a child. Messiah will be begotten by God—yet He will be God. He will be

---

* Harry Houdini, perhaps the greatest magician that ever lived, once gave a demonstration in Paris of his ability to unlock locks. A local magician claimed he could do all that Houdini did. And he publicly offered to extricate himself the next day from a cage, locked by Houdini's special lock. The wily French magician had an accomplice, unknown to Houdini, who wormed the combination of the lock from the American magician. But Houdini suspected the trick—so that night he changed the combination. The next day the cocky French magician had himself locked in the cage. To his chagrin, he could not unlock the combination lock. He tried in vain to discover the new combination, midst the jeers of the crowd. Finally, he had to beg Houdini to release him, which he did after a little showmanship. Then Houdini showed him and the audience what the new five-letter combination was: F-R-A-U-D. The one who worked out the combination is the one who could unlock it. The One who gave these mysterious Old Testament prophecies, as a LOCK, knows the combination that unlocks the mysteries, and He alone knows them. Jesus had the "key" in His own Person and ministry that unlocks them! All counterfeit "Messiahs" are frauds!

a "Son" in time—yet He is "Father of Eternity" (Isa. 9:6). Chosen by God, elect, precious—yet despised and rejected by men, He is a "man of sorrows and acquainted with grief." Coming to the Jews, and rejected by them as a nation—He will be sought by the Gentiles and will be a "light to the Gentiles." He will be a man who is God—and God who is man. Sinless, and having a wholly benevolent ministry—He will eventually be forsaken by both God and man. He will be "abhorred"—yet extolled and exalted. "Cut off"—yet His days will be prolonged. "Grief and glory, travail and triumph, humiliation and exaltation, cross and crown are so strongly intermingled that the ancient Jewish expositors could not reconcile these prophecies. The whole prophetic picture of the coming Messiah, with its fulfillment, is so wholly novel, so mysterious, so artless and yet so intricate, that it was and is and must for ever remain the wonder of all literature" (A. T. Pierson).

Let us examine in more detail a few of the many prophetic paradoxes in the predictions of the coming Messiah.

(1) **Concerning His birth.** Notice in the following predictions these striking irreconcilables: a **virgin** . . . shall bear a son: something unknown in human experience. And this manchild will be GOD—"God with us." God-begotten—yet God incarnate!

"The Lord Himself shall give you a sign; Behold, a virgin shall conceive, and bear a son, and shall call his name IMMANUEL" (Isa. 7:14).

"For unto us a child is born, unto us a Son is given: and the government shall be upon His shoulder: and His name shall be called Wonderful (Heb., miracle), Counsellor, the Mighty God, the Father of Eternity, the Prince of Peace" (Isa. 9:6).

To fulfill these amazing prophecies God performed a "biological miracle" and Christ was conceived by the Holy Spirit (Luke 1:35) and born of the virgin Mary as recorded in Matthew 1:16-25. To fulfill these two predictions quoted above, given 700 years before their fulfillment, God in the person of His Son came to earth, and the incarnation became a reality: "the Son of the Highest" became Mary's son: God manifest in the flesh (see 1 Tim. 3:16; John 1:1-3,14; Luke 1:31-33) —and all this though Mary "knew not a man" (Luke 1:34).

Not only was Messiah to be the GOD-MAN, born of a virgin

(Isa. 7:14; Isa. 9:6), He was in some mysterious way to be all of these: "the Seed of the woman" (Gen. 3:15); "the Son of man" (Dan. 7:13); the "Son of God" (Ps. 2:7); the "Seed of Abraham" (Gen. 22:18); and the "fruit" of David's body (Ps. 132:11). But how can God be man and man be God and at the same time be a son of man and Son of God? And how can a person be God and yet be born of God? And how can one be a "son of man" and yet have no human father? And how can he be the "seed of the woman" when the woman "knew not a man?" How in the world—pardon the expression —could one person be ALL these? Wonder of wonders, Jesus was! The Lord Jesus was GOD (John 1:1); He was man (John 1:14); He was the "seed of the woman" (Gal. 4:4); He was the "Son of man"—the representative man (Luke 19:10); He was the "Son of God" (John 3:16); He was the "seed of Abraham and the seed of David" (Matt. 1:1). Behold, the Miracle of the ages: Christ Jesus, perfect man, yet very God; God begotten, yet God incarnate in one indivisible, loving, matchless personality! John the evangelist explains the supreme mystery (called the "mystery of God and of Christ," Col. 2:2; 4:3) in these words:

"And the Word (who was God and was with God, in the bosom of the Father) was made flesh, and dwelt among us; and we beheld His glory, the glory as of the only begotten of the Father, full of grace and truth" (see John 1:1-2,18,14).

(2) **The Place of His Origin: from whence did He come: Bethlehem? Egypt? Nazareth?** Here is another involved series of predictions. Prophecy said, "Out of thee (Bethlehem) shall he come forth . . . who is to be ruler in Israel" (Mic. 5:2). But another Scripture said, "I have called my Son out of Egypt" (Hos. 11:1 with Matt. 2:15). And there was a spoken prophecy commonly known among the people of Israel, as one of the predictions of the prophets, "He shall be called a Nazarene" (Matt. 2:23), based possibly on Isaiah 11:1, where Messiah is called the Branch (Heb., **neh-tzer**), meaning the separated One, or "the Nazarene."

Are these contradictory? Not at all when the Person came who unlocked the puzzle by the course of events in His divinely ordained life. He was **born** in Bethlehem, as Micah said; soon after, He was taken to Egypt by Joseph and Mary, from whence God "called" Him back to the Holy Land after the death of wicked king Herod (Matt. 2:13-23). And when Joseph and Mary came back to Palestine with the child Jesus, they settled in Nazareth, the city where the Lord was reared.* Hence, in His ministry He was called "Jesus of Nazareth" (Luke 18:37; Acts 2:22; etc.). Isn't it strange that, though He was born in Bethlehem, no one ever calls Him "Jesus of Bethlehem," and though He is called "Jesus of Nazareth," everyone knows He was born in Bethlehem, not Nazareth!

Being of the tribe of Judah, and born in Bethlehem, He was indeed a true "Nazarene," a "separated one," by living in Galilee instead of with his Judean brethren in Judah! Even as Joseph of old also was separated ("Nazared") from his brethren by his exile for so many years in Egypt (see Gen. 49:26, where the word "separate" comes from the Hebrew root **nazar**).

The historical record of the life of Jesus makes crystal clear these three apparently contradictory prophecies.

(3) How could Messiah be both David's Son . . . yet David's Lord? Christ Himself raised this interesting question with the Pharisees, when He asked them pointedly:

"What think ye of Christ? whose son is He? They say unto him, The Son of David. He saith unto them, How then doth David in Spirit call Him Lord, saying, The Lord said unto my Lord, Sit Thou on My right hand, till I make thine enemies Thy footstool? If David then called Him Lord, how is He his Son?" (Matt. 22:41-45; Christ quoted from Psalm 110:1).

------

* There is an interesting historical sidelight that adds pungency to the understanding of the prediction and its fulfillment. When Joseph and Mary returned to the holy land, from Egypt, Joseph was apparently about to settle near Bethlehem, in Judea; "but when he heard that Archelaus did reign in Judea in the room of his father Herod, he was afraid to go thither: . . . he turned aside into the parts of Galilee: and he came and dwelt in a city called Nazareth: that it might be fulfilled which was spoken by the prophets, He shall be called a Nazarene" (Matt. 2:22-23). Humanly speaking, all hinged on this queer fact: In a peevish fret, before his death, king Herod changed his will and put Archelaus, the worst of his living sons, to rule instead of Antipas. It was this fear of Archelaus that led Joseph to look for another residence; then God led him to Nazareth! So God, who uses the wrath of man to praise Him, permitted the wrath of a petulant king to bring to pass a fulfillment of His Word! (See Ps. 76:10).

Is it hard to see how Christ could be both David's son and David's Lord? Not at all when one has the key to the problem in the facts as presented in the New Testament. Christ was David's son in that He was a descendant of David, after the flesh (Luke 1:32; Rom. 1:3); and He was David's Lord, for Messiah is God: King of kings and Lord of all (Rev. 19:16). Messiah is called LORD (Jehovah) in Jeremiah 23:6, and He is called GOD (Elohim) in Psalm 45:6 (cf. Heb. 1:8), and He is called Lord (Adonai) in Malachi 3:1 and Psalm 110:1—all three names and titles of Deity in the Old Testament. It is clear, Messiah is not only David's Lord, but He is LORD OF ALL.

(4) **Christ's Right to David's Throne.** Here is an intricate, involved puzzle: so involved it will take a little concentration on the part of the reader to follow the problem and its solution—but it will well repay the effort.

Christ, the Seed of David, must be virgin-born, and yet have a legal right to the throne of David despite the fact that one of Solomon's descendants was a certain evil man named Jeconiah, of whom it was written that none of his descendants would ever rule in Judah (see Jerem. 22:29-30); and despite the fact that in Israel **the right to the throne was transmitted only through the male line:** and here Christ was born of a virgin!

It is perfectly clear that Messiah will inherit "the throne of David" (Isa. 9:7; Jerem. 33:15-17; 25:5; Ps. 132:11; 1 Chron. 17:11,14). But, since He had to be born of a virgin, **how can He get His legal right to the throne of David?** And how can the roadblock erected by Jeconiah's sin be circumvented? Who can untangle these apparently hopelessly confused predictions? Leave it to the Master Mind who both devised the strange prophecies and worked out their fulfillment. Remember, the prophet Isaiah said, "The zeal of the Lord of Hosts shall perform this" (Isa. 9:7).

Not only was the apparently impossible solved and resolved in JESUS THE CHRIST, but God has given us the complete record of how He did it in the genealogies of the New Testament. In Matthew's genealogy the genealogy of Christ through **Joseph** is given. This genealogy shows Christ to be "the son of

David"—so giving Him right to David's throne—and also "the son of Abraham"—so giving Him right to the Land of Promise, the territorial possessions givn to Abraham and his seed.*

In Matthew's genealogy, Joseph is seen to be in the REGAL line of descent from king David, down through Solomon. But Joseph was also a descendant of David through Jeconiah (also called Coniah)—hence, succession to the throne for Joseph personally is barred. Matthew's genealogical record is careful to show that Jesus was NOT, through Joseph, the "fruit of David's body," i. e., a direct descendant of David through Joseph.

In Luke 3:23-38 Christ's genealogy is given through Mary. (Heli was obviously Mary's father, Joseph's father-in-law, v. 23).** In the record Christ is shown to be the LITERAL "fruit of David's body" through His mother Mary. But, and this is important: while Mary was in A ROYAL line from David, she was not in THE REGAL lineage, for she was a descendant of king David through Nathan, whereas the throne rights were to come through Solomon's line (see 1 Chron. 28:5-6). Therefore, Joseph's marriage to Mary before Christ was born was an absolute necessity—and that is exactly what happened!

"Now the birth of Jesus Christ was on this wise: When as his mother Mary was espoused to Joseph, before they came together, she was found with child of the Holy Spirit. . . . And behold the angel of the Lord appeared unto him in a dream, saying, Joseph, thou SON OF DAVID, fear

---

* It is interesting to observe that in Luke (3:38) the genealogy of Christ is traced back through Heli (Mary's father) to ADAM and to GOD—so giving Christ a title-deed to the whole earth, as "son of Adam" (see Gen. 1:27-30; Ps. 8:4-6; Heb. 2:6-9; Rev. 5:1-10) and to "ALL THINGS" as "Son of God" (see Hebrews 1:2).

** It is interesting to note that in the genealogical record in Matthew, it is written that "Jacob begat Joseph" (Matt. 1:16); that is, Jacob was the actual father of Joseph. But in Luke it is written that "Joseph was the son of Heli" (Luke 3:23), and the word "son" is not in the original, but is supplied by the translators. In this verse (Luke 3:23) it should be "son-in-law" instead of son. Obviously, Joseph could not have two fathers —hence, he is the "son-in-law" of Heli, or the "son" in the sense that he is married to Heli's daughter. This is in accordance with Jewish custom (see 1 Sam. 24:16).

not to take unto thee Mary THY WIFE: for that which is conceived in her is of the Holy Spirit" (Matt. 1:18-20).*

So, through Mary, Jesus the Christ obtained His **literal** descent from king David; and from Mary's marriage to Joseph, who was also a "son of David," He obtained His **legal** right to David's throne, for Mary was Joseph's **wife** before Jesus was born, so making Joseph Jesus' legal father, His foster father. And, withal, the prophecy concerning Jeconiah was fulfilled too, for Jesus the Christ is NOT the "seed"—a direct descendant—of Jeconiah. Can you think of anything more intricate and involved, and yet worked out with such precision?

Joseph and Mary **had** to be the parents (foster father and mother) of Jesus the Christ: they were the only two people of that generation who could be, and fulfill prophecy about Messiah. And Joseph **had** to be married to Mary before Jesus was born, so He could get His legal right to David's throne through Joseph. At the same time, Christ could not be a child of Joseph because of the bar against a descendant of Jeconiah. And though Joseph had to be married to Mary, yet Joseph could not "know" Mary as his wife until after Jesus was born, for He had to be born of a virgin! And the Divinely ordered fulfillment was perfect in every detail!

(5) Messiah was to be Both the "Chief Corner Stone" and the "Rock of Offence."

"He shall be . . . for a stone of stumbling and for a rock of offence to both the houses of Israel" (Isa. 8:14).

"The stone which the builders refused is become the head stone of the corner" (Ps. 118:22; Isa. 28:16).

The key that unlocks this mystery is a simple one: **belief or unbelief in Christ.** To those who disbelieve, Messiah would be a "Rock of Offence" and a "Stone of Stumbling." Peter ex-

---

* It is a mistake to minimize the importance of the genealogical records of the Bible. They are of prime importance in proving that Jesus of Nazareth is MESSIAH and that He has the right to the throne of David. Incidentally, the presence of the genealogical records in the New Testament shows the importance God places on the PROOF that Jesus is David's Son, and indirectly shows the importance of the whole argument from fulfilled prophecy.

plains the mystery by showing that all depends on one's attitude toward Christ, whether of faith or unbelief:

"Wherefore also it is contained in the Scripture, Behold, I lay in Zion a chief corner stone, elect, precious: and he that believeth on Him shall not be confounded. Unto you therefore which believe He is precious: but unto them which be disobedient, the stone which the builders disallowed the same is made the head of the corner. And a stone of stumbling, and a rock of offence, even to them which stumble at the word, being disobedient" (1 Pet. 2:6-8). See also Romans 9:32-33.

As He did so often, the Lord Jesus called attention to the prophecy in the Old Testament, making Himself the New Testament fulfilment of it.

"Jesus saith unto them (the Pharisees), Did ye never read in the Scriptures, The stone which the builders rejected, the same is become the head of the corner: this is the Lord's doing, and it is marvelous in our eyes" (Matt. 21:42). The Lord also added this significant statement: "And whosoever shall fall on this stone"—seeking His mercy and grace—"shall be broken"—his hopes in himself completely crushed. "But on whomsoever it shall fall"—in judgment—"it will grind him to powder"—completely ruin him for time and eternity. (See Matt. 22:44).

To the believer, Christ is the CHIEF CORNER STONE, and He is very precious. To the unbeliever, Christ is the STONE OF STUMBLING or ROCK OF OFFENCE. To the one, Christ the Rock brings eternal salvation; to the other, He brings judgment. Those who stumble in unbelief over Christ reject Him and fall to their eternal destruction.

(6) Rejected by Israel (Isa. 53:3), Messiah would then become "a Light to the Gentiles" for "Salvation unto the end of the earth" (Isa. 49:5,6).

Racially, Messiah would be a Jew (a "Branch" out of the stem of Jesse, Isa. 11:1,10); and yet, the Gentiles will seek Him (Isa. 11:10)—an unheard of thing, for there is and has been for ages a natural animosity between Jews and Gentiles. But this enmity is done away "in Christ" (Eph. 2:14,15).

The veil over the hearts of the Gentiles will be destroyed for multitudes of believing Gentiles (see Isa. 25:7), and a veil of unbelief will form over the hearts of many (not all) Jews. Isaiah predicted this judicial blindness for Israel, because they "despised and rejected" their Messiah.

"Make the heart of this people (Israel) fat, and make their ears heavy, and shut their eyes; lest they . . . convert, and be healed" (Isa. 6:10).

"It is a light thing that thou shouldest be My Servant . . . to restore the preserved of Israel; I will also give thee for a light to the Gentiles, that Thou mayest be my salvation unto the end of the earth" (Isa. 49:6).

Nineteen centuries of history attest the truth of these words. When Israel crucified and rejected their Messiah, a veil of unbelief settled over the nation, and though some believe in the Lord Jesus and are saved, blindness is still over the hearts and minds of most Israelites (2 Cor. 3:14,15). The Gospel was then given to the Gentiles (see Acts 28:28), and the glorious gospel in John 3:16 is now preached to the whole world, Jew and Gentile alike. That Gentiles should trust in a Jew for salvation is most unlikely, but true. That the very nation He came to bless turned from Him seems most unlikely, but it happened (John 1:11,12); and that the Gentiles who were not the people of God should become the people of God through faith in the Jewish Messiah seems preposterous—but that is the way God is working and that is the way it is happening.

(7) **Messiah was to have a DOUBLE ANOINTING—A Ministry of Mercy as Saviour, and a Ministry of Judgment, as Coming King.**

Since Christ at His first advent came to suffer for the sins of the people we now know (though the Jews of Jesus' day found it hard to realize this) that His role as JUDGE and KING will be fulfilled at His **second** advent.

"Isaiah who describes with the eloquence worthy of a prophet the glories of Messiah's coming kingdom, also characterizes with the accuracy of the historian the humiliation, the trials, the agony, which were to precede the triumph of the Redeemer of the world," says W. G. Moorehead, "presenting on the one hand a glorious King, Himself Deity, 'God with us,' who has all power; yet, on the other hand, One whose visage was more marred than any man, His bones out of joint and dying of thirst (Ps. 22). How can He be both the great Davidic Monarch, restoring again the glory of Solomon's House, and also be a Sacrifice bearing the sins of the people? Clearly, destinies so strongly contrasted **could not be accomplished simultaneously.** There is only one answer possible; . . . in the Divine purpose the mighty drama is to be IN TWO ACTS (His first advent and His second advent)."

The "suffering" Messiah (and His ministry of mercy) is often presented in the same Scripture with His work as Judge and King. In the Scripture we quote below we print in CAPS the phrase that describes His work of judging at His second advent. The rest applies to His first advent.

"The Spirit of the Lord God is upon Me; because the Lord hath anointed Me to preach good tidings unto the meek; He hath sent Me to bind up the broken-hearted, to proclaim liberty to the captives, and the opening of the prison to them that are bound; to proclaim the acceptable year of the Lord, AND THE DAY OF VENGEANCE OF OUR GOD" (Isa. 61:1-2).

The same intermingling of prophecy describing Messiah's work at both advents—to save and to judge; His humiliation and work as the Redeemer at His first advent, and His work to establish His righteous kingdom at His second advent—is seen in many other Scriptures, such as Zechariah 9: 9-10; Micah 5:1-4; Daniel 9:24, etc.

In studying Messianic prophecy, it is important to determine if the first or second advent, or both advents, are in view.

When Christ in the synagogue at Capernaum applied this Scripture in Isaiah (61:1-2) to Himself (see Luke 4:17-21) He stopped His reading with the words, ". . . to proclaim the acceptable year of the Lord." Why? He will NOT proclaim the **Day of vengeance of our God** until His second advent.

The ancient Rabbis, studying these and similar predictions about the coming Messiah, came to the conclusion there must be TWO MESSIAHS: One a suffering, the other a conquering, judging Messiah. They failed to see this great truth, even as most of Israel to this day has likewise failed, that there is only ONE MESSIAH, the Lord Jesus Christ, who has two distinct tasks to perform: One at His first advent, "to make reconciliation for iniquity" and the second when He returns to earth at His second advent as the mighty King: "to bring in everlasting righteousness" (Dan. 9:24). In Christ, the scores of apparently contradictory Messianic prophecies that refer either to His first advent or to His second advent, with their different objectives, are fully harmonized. These two advents of Christ are in contrast in such passages as Isaiah 53 and Isaiah 11; Psalm 22 and Psalm 72; Psalm 69 and Psalm 89. This same truth is fully revealed in the New Testament in such passages as 1 Peter 1:11, which speaks of "the sufferings of Christ" at His first advent and "the glory that should follow" at His second advent. Contrast also John 3:16,17 with Revelation 19:11-21; Luke 9:56 with Jude 14,15 and Luke 19:10 with 2 Thessalonians 1:7-10.

(8) Messiah will be a "Priest upon His Throne."

"Thus speaketh the Lord of hosts, saying, Behold the man whose name is the BRANCH . . . He shall build the temple of the Lord . . . He shall be a priest upon His throne" (Zech. 6:12-13).

In Psalm 110:4 Messiah is called "a priest for ever after the order of Melchizedek." In Jeremiah 23:5 Messiah is called "the righteous Branch a King." In the history of Israel the chosen line of kings always came from the tribe of Judah (except among the Ten Tribes of Israel). Priests came from the tribe of Levi. Since Christ was from the Tribe of Judah (Heb. 7:14) how could He also be a priest, since He could not come from two tribes (Judah and Levi)?

How was the puzzle solved? Christ is a King from the tribe of Judah; He will sit upon His throne on earth at His second advent. Christ also is a Priest whose priesthood is **patterned** after the Aaronic priesthood in which the priests offered sacrifices for the sins of the people (and Christ offered Himself as the once-for-all Sacrifice for sin, Heb. 9:26). But He was **made** a priest after the **order** of Melchizedek (Heb. 5:6; Ps. 110:4) who was both a king and a priest (Heb. 7:1-2). This whole intriguing subject of Christ's priesthood is fully explained in Hebrews 7, 8, and 9. So, the mystery is solved in Christ!

(9) Messiah, the Chosen Servant of the Lord, would be a Lovely Character most pleasing to God, His "elect in whom His Soul delighted" (Isa. 42.1); yet this "Holy One" would be "abhored" by the Nation Israel (Isa. 49:7).

Isaiah 40:5 tells us that in Messiah, the Coming One, the "glory of the Lord" shall be revealed, and all flesh shall see it. Then, in complete contrast, Messiah is spoken of as the One who would be "despised and rejected of men" in whom the nation will see "no beauty" that they should desire Him (Isa. 53:1-3).

In the history of Jesus the paradox is explained. The Father said of Jesus, His Beloved One, "this is My beloved Son in whom I am well pleased" (Matt. 17:5). On the other hand, the people rejected Him; and no prophecies than those that tell of His rejection ever received a sadder fulfillment. The pathos of Messiah's rejection is told by Jesus Himself:

"O Jerusalem, Jerusalem, that killest the prophets, and stonest them which are sent unto thee, how often would I have gathered thy children together, even as a hen gathereth her chickens under her wings, and ye would not" (Matt. 23:37).

They that "hated Him without a cause" were "more than the hairs of his head" (Ps. 69:4; John 15:25). The New Testament record tells us that "He came unto His own and His own received Him not" (John 1:11).

(10) "Thirty Pieces of Silver"—the Price of Christ or the Price of the Potter's Field?

"And I said unto them, If ye think good, give Me My price; and if not, forbear. So they weighed for My price thirty pieces of silver. And the Lord said unto Me, Cast it unto the potter: a goodly price that I was prized at of them. And I took the thirty pieces of silver, and cast them to the potter in the house of the Lord" (Zech. 11:12,13)

Strange words indeed that one would have difficulty in understanding or reconciling with any specific event in history, **were it not for the fulfillment as given in the New Testament,** where we read that Judas covenanted with the chief priests to betray Christ and deliver Him to them: "and they covenanted with him for thirty pieces of silver" (Matt. 26:15). When the heinousness of his crime dawned on Judas, he

"brought the thirty pieces of silver to the chief priests and elders . . . and he cast down the pieces of silver in the temple . . . and went out and hanged himself . . . And the chief priests took the silver pieces . . . and they took counsel and bought with them the potter's field. . . . Then was fulfilled that which was spoken by Jeremiah the prophet, saying, And they took the thirty pieces of silver, the price of Him that was valued . . . and gave them for the potter's field" (Matt. 27:3-10).

Not only Judas, but the nation Israel sold Christ and **woefully underestimated Him.** They sold Him for thirty pieces of silver, the price of a dead slave (Ex. 21:32); and so the Jewish leaders expressed their hatred for and contempt of the Holy One. Here is the perfect example of "the certain degree of obscurity" in some prophecies that is "unveiled in the fulfillment."

"No one can suppose that the perfect agreement of the Old Testament prediction with its New Testament fulfillment, centering about the exact amount of the sum of money (30 pieces of silver) could be accidental. Still less can it be conceived that the appropriation of the money to the purchase of the Potter's field could have taken place without an overruling design" (Book of Prophecy, pp. 343-344). In the fulfillment, all obscurity is removed and the perfect harmony of the fulfillment with the prophecy is seen. "It was so exactly fulfilled that every one can see that the same God who spoke through the prophet had, by the secret operation of His omnipotent power, which extends even to the ungodly, so arranged matters that when Judas threw back their money and the chief priests purchased the potter's field, they (not only fulfilled prophecy, but) perpetuated the memorial of their sin against their Messiah, and called forth the vengeance of God against their nation."*

(11) **Prophecy presents the Messiah as not only rejected by Men, but forsaken by God too; horrible Sufferings and Death would come to the One who perfectly obeyed God at all times.**

In Psalm 22:1 Messiah prophetically ejaculates, "My God, My God, why hast Thou forsaken Me?" The desolate cry of the One forsaken by God as well as by man is repeated in the New Testament, while Jesus was being crucified.

"And about the ninth hour Jesus cried with a loud voice, saying . My God, My God, why hast Thou forsaken Me?" (Matt. 27:46).

God "hath made Him (Christ) to be sin for us, who knew no sin; that we might be made the righteousness of God in Him" (2 Cor. 5:21).

This forsaking of the Righteous One in whom God delighted (Ps. 22:8), is all the more strange, for from the beginning of human history "the fathers (who) trusted in God . . . where delivered" (Ps. 22:4-5)—but not so in THIS instance. The strange enigma is only fully understood by the explanation of the New Testament that in the sufferings and death of Christ on the cross, God turned away from Christ, for:

God "made Him (Christ) to be sin for us, who knew no sin; that we might be made the righteousness of God in Him" (2 Cor. 5:21).

(12) **"Wounded" and "Pierced"—yet "not a Bone broken,"** is the amazing prophetic record of the Coming Messiah. He was to be "wounded in the house of His friends" (Zech. 13:6), with both "hands and feet pierced" (Ps. 22:16)—yet in some miraculous way not a bone of the suffering Messiah was to be broken. In the Psalms Jehovah said of Messiah, "He keepeth all His bones: not one of them is broken" (Ps. 34:20; cf. Ex. 12:46).

---

* David Baron, in "Visions and Prophecies of Zechariah," p. 409.

At the crucifixion, when the Jews feared that the three who were being crucified might linger on until death came too late to remove their bodies from the crosses before the Sabbath, they sought permission from Pilate that "their legs might be broken"—an act to hasten death, that they might be removed sooner from the crosses.

"Then came the soldiers and brake the legs of the first, and the other which was crucified with Him; but when they came to Jesus, and saw that He was dead already they brake not His legs: but one of the soldiers with a spear pierced His side, and forthwith came there out blood and water. And he that saw it bare record, and his record is true: for these things were done, that the Scripture might be fulfilled, a bone of Him shall not be broken. And again another Scripture saith, They shall look on Him whom they pierced" (John 19:31-37).

Marvelous miracle of Divine Providence: they broke the legs of two of those who were crucified, but NOT of the third; for prophecy had said, "not a bone of Him shall be broken." They pierced His hands, His feet and His side, and each time the weapons went between the bones and did not break them.

(13) **Messiah who was to be "cut off"** (Dan. 9:26; Isa. 53: 8), **and who "poured out His Soul unto Death"** (Ps. 53:12), **was also to be "exalted and extolled and be very High"** (Isa. 52:13); **and God shall "prolong His Days, and the Pleasure of the Lord shall prosper in His Hand"** (Isa. 53:10), **and God "shall divide Him a Portion with the Great"** (Isa. 53:12).

And so the glorious facts of Messiah's atoning death and resurrection are prophetically stated in language clear when fulfilled but obscure until fulfilled, in one of the most thrilling prophetic paradoxes in the whole realm of Scripture.

In the New Testament we read that Jesus

"humbled Himself, and became obedient unto death, even the death of the cross. Wherefore, God also hath highly exalted Him, and given Him a name which is above every name: that at the name of Jesus every knee should bow . . . and every tongue should confess that Jesus Christ is LORD to the glory of God the Father" (Phil. 2:9-11).

Man despised Him and set Him at nought (Isa. 53:3); but in His time God will make Him "higher than the kings of the earth" (Ps. 89:27). Both Old Testament prophets and readers puzzled over this mystery (see 1 Peter 1:10-11), but all was made plain when Jesus the Christ in the New Testament died for our sins, and was raised from the dead on the third day.

IV. PROPHECIES CONCERNING THE SUFFERINGS, DEATH AND RESURRECTION OF MESSIAH. An Examination of (1) Psalm 22; (2) Isaiah 53.

(1) PSALM 22

THE MIRACLE OF THE TWENTY-SECOND PSALM is this: Crucifixion was a Roman and a Grecian custom, unknown to the Jews until the days of their captivity (600 B.C.). The Jews executed their criminals by **stoning**. And yet, written one thousand years before the time of Christ, by a man who had never seen or heard of such a method of execution as crucifixion, Psalm 22 gives a graphic portrayal of death by crucifixion!

The Messianic nature of this Psalm is almost universally admitted by devout students.

"Psalm 22," said D. M. Panton, "one of David's Psalms, reveals someone—Messiah—dying an awful death, under very peculiar circumstances. The ancient document says, 'The assembly of evil-doers have inclosed Me: they pierced My hands and My feet. I may tell all my bones; they look and stare upon Me' (v. 16). Crucifixion in David's time was unknown among the Jews; yet the piercing of hands and feet together with the partial stripping—'telling all the bones'—obviously means crucifixion: the crucified are pierced only in their hands and feet, and stripped for exposure. WOULD A FALSE MESSIAH HAVE CHOSEN THIS PASSAGE FOR FULFILLMENT? This old document (Ps. 22) holds the very crucifixion cry, for the Psalm opens with it—'My God, my God, why hast Thou forsaken Me?' (v. 1). Not a jot or tittle of this Psalm has miscarried: exactly as in His birth and in His ministry, so also in His death—but more so—the ancient document is a photograph of the fact, fulfilled in flawless detail." (Dawn Magazine).

The Forsaken One

Christ on the cross identified Himself with the One spoken of in this Psalm by quoting its first verse: "My God, My God, why hast Thou forsaken Me?" (Matt. 27:46). This Psalm has been called "The Psalm of Sobs."*

"The Hebrew shows not one completed sentence in the opening verses, but a series of brief ejaculations, like the gasps of a dying man whose breath and strength are failing, and who can only utter a word or two at a time: 'My God—My God—why forsaken Me—far from helping Me—words of My roaring'—presenting a picture overwhelmingly pathetic: the

---

* Bishop Alexander in, "Witness of the Psalms to Christ."

suffering Saviour, forsaken by God, gasping for life, unable to articulate one continuous sentence. . . . The writer thus forecasts the mystery of the cross which remained unsolved for a thousand years. It was like a dark cavern at the time, but when the Gospel narrative portrays Jesus as the Crucified One, it is like putting a lighted torch in the cavern."[*]

Periods of Light and Darkness

In verse 2 one sees alternate periods of light and darkness:

"O my God, I cry in the daytime but Thou hearest not; and in the night season, and am not silent" (Ps. 22:2).

In the New Testament account of the crucifixion of Christ, we read:

"Now from the sixth hour there was darkness over all the land unto the ninth hour" (Matt. 27:45).

Righteous—yet Forsaken by God

In verses 3 to 5 we see a prophetic discussion of this strange anomaly: a truly Righteous One forsaken by God. It never happened so before in the history of the "fathers": **they** trusted, and were delivered; Messiah on the cross is **forsaken.** Christ on the Cross was forsaken by God and man.

They Mocked Him

Verses 6 to 8 tell of those who reproached and mocked Him:

They "laugh Me to scorn: they shoot out the lips, they shake the head, saying, He trusted on the Lord: let Him deliver Him, seeing He delighted in Him" (v. 8).

The New Testament tells us how the people ridiculed and derided Christ on the cross (see Matthew 27:39-44), using almost the identical words the prophet used:

"Likewise also the chief priests mocking him said . . . He trusted in God; let him deliver him now" (Matt. 27:41, 43).

His Weakness, Thirst and exposure to Public Scorn

In the prophetic record, further startling details are given:

The people "gaped upon Me . . . I am poured out like water, and all my bones are out of joint: my heart is like wax: it is melted in the midst of my bowels. My strength is dried up like a potsherd; and my tongue cleaveth to my jaws; and thou hast brought me into the dust of death" (vs. 13-15).

Messiah's exposure to public scorn—"they gaped upon Me" (v. 13)—was fulfilled in New Testament times, at the cross,

---

[*] A. T. Pierson, in "Living Oracles," p. 107.

when the people "sitting down . . . watched Him" (Matthew 27:36). His extreme weakness, perspiration and thirst, under the pitiless beating of the oriental sun, are predicted:

"I am poured out like water . . . my strength is dried up like a potsherd; and my tongue cleaveth to my jaws" (vs. 14, 15).

The forsaken Sufferer in the New Testament expressed in one simple statement His weakness and thirst:

"After this, Jesus knowing that all things were now accomplished, that the Scripture might be fulfilled, saith, I thirst" (John 19:28).

He Died of a Broken Heart

One weeps in heart, thinking of Messiah's horrible sufferings: such as the agony from dislocated bones, caused by the weight of the body suspended only by the nails in the hands and feet: "all my bones are out of joint" (v. 14). Add to that the mental and spiritual torture so great it literally broke His heart: "My heart is melted in the midst of my bowels" (v. 14). At last, His sufferings were ended by death: "Thou hast brought me into the dust of death" (v. 15).

There is evidence from the New Testament record that Christ died of a broken heart. When the Roman soldier "pierced His side" (John 19:34) "forthwith came there out blood and water," indicating that the heart had been ruptured (before it was pierced by the Roman spear), probably from the great emotional strain Christ had been under. The lymphatic fluid apparently had separated from the red blood, producing "blood and water." The word "lymph" comes from the Latin **lympha**, meaning water. See also 1 John 5:6.

The Parting of His Garments

"They part my garments among them, and cast lots upon my vesture" (v. 18).

For exquisite detail, dramatically fulfilled, this is the gem of all prophecy. The divinely inspired prophet, looking down through ten centuries of time, sees and records an incident connected with the crucifixion that seems so trivial and unimportant one wonders why it is referred to at all—unless it be to let us know that Omniscience wrote the prophecy and Omnipotence fulfilled it.

In the New Testament account of the crucifixion of Christ —when they "pierced His hands and His feet"—that additional, "unimportant" detail about the disposition of Messiah's garments is mentioned. Roman soldiers, ignorant of both God and prophecy, and knowing nothing of the sacred import of what they were doing, **fulfilled to the letter that age-old prediction!**

"Then the soldiers, when they had crucified Jesus, took His garments and made four parts, to every soldier a part; and also His coat: now the coat was without seam, woven from the top throughout. They said therefore among themselves, Let us not rend it, but cast lots for it, whose it shall be; **that the Scripture might be fulfilled** which saith, They parted my raiment among them, and for my vesture they did cast lots" (John 19:23-24).

And so an obscure prophecy, hidden in the Old Testament for a thousand years, springs forth as a witness, a living miracle, proving again that GOD SPAKE in the Old Testament and GOD FULFILLED in the New Testament. This one prophecy is enough to convince the most skeptical, if he have an honest heart, that the predictions concerning Messiah in the Old Testament were fulfilled in the Christ of the Gospels, so giving a satisfying demonstration of the Divine origin of both Testaments.

The Resurrection of Messiah

This Messiah, so cruelly put to death, will be "helped" (v. 19), "delivered" (v. 20), "saved from the lion's mouth" (v. 21). His prayer will be "answered" (v. 21: "Thou hast answered Me," RV). Verse 21 is the end of a section. Verse 22 begins a new section; and Messiah now gloriously delivered, resurrected, says:

"I will declare Thy name unto my brethren: in the midst of the congregation will I praise thee" (v. 22).

The New Testament of course bears abundant evidence that though Christ died, forsaken by God and man, yet **God raised Him from the dead on the third day.**

"Ye have taken (Christ), and by wicked hands have crucified and slain (Him): Whom GOD HATH RAISED UP, having loosed the pangs of death: because it was not possible that he should be holden of it" (Acts 2:23, 24).

A Summary

"The predictions concerning Christ in this chapter," writes Moses Margoliouth, "are so numerous and so minute that they could not possibly have been dictated by any but by Him to whom all things are naked and open, and who worketh all things according to the counsel of His own will. The most **insignificant** circumstances connected with our Lord's death are set forth with as much accuracy as those which are **most important** . . . What could be more unlikely than that Messiah should be crucified when crucifixion was not a Jewish but a Roman punishment? And yet David in this Psalm predicted such would be the case centuries before Rome was founded" and ten centuries before the prophecy was fulfilled!

(2) ISAIAH 53

THIS REMARKABLE PROPHECY of the sufferings and exaltation of Messiah was written 700 years before the time of Christ. It reads more like "an historical summary of the Gospel narrative of the sufferings of Christ and the glory that should follow, instead of a prophecy" (David Baron). With this agrees Augustine, who said, "Methinks Isaiah writes not a prophecy but a Gospel." And another commentator says, "It reads as if it had been written beneath the cross of Golgotha. It is the deepest and the loftiest thing that Old Testament prophecy, outstripping itself, has ever achieved."

"This chapter," says A. T. Pierson*, "is a bundle of paradoxes, or apparent contradictions, as numerous as the verses in the chapter. In fact, it was DESIGNED to present a prophetic enigma which only the Person (and work) of the Christ of the New Testament can solve. He is a root out of the dry ground—yet fruitful; He has no form nor beauty—yet He is the chosen Servant of God; He is despised and rejected of men— yet He is the appointed Saviour; He suffers unto death—yet He survives; He has no offspring—yet He has a numerous seed; men would make His grave with the wicked—yet He is buried with the rich; He suffers unbelievable adversity—yet He enjoys prosperity; He is triumphed over— yet He triumphs; He is condemned—yet He justifies the condemned. These paradoxes remained a problem until the cross was set up, the sepulchre burst open, and the Son of God who came to die went up to reign."

Unfortunately, the chapter division comes at the wrong place. It should begin with Isaiah 52:13, which starts with the words, "BEHOLD MY SERVANT" . . . and that is the subject of this entire section, Isaiah 52:13—53:12. It is a graphic portrayal of

The Suffering Messiah . . . "Jehovah's Servant"

The first question to be answered is, "Of whom speaketh

* Living Oracles, p. 110.

the prophet? of himself, or of some other?" (Acts 8:34). The only possible correct answer is, This prophecy speaks of an individual, MESSIAH,* and there is only One Person in the history of the world whom it fits: Christ of the New Testament.

"Let any one steep his mind in the contents of this chapter," observes Professor James Orr, "and then read what is said about Jesus in the Gospels, and as he stands underneath the Cross, see if there is not the most perfect correspondence between the two. In Jesus of Nazareth alone in all history, but in Him perfectly, has this prophecy found fulfillment."

We wish now to call attention in more detail to some of the prophetic wonders, descriptions of Messiah's rejection, sufferings, death, resurrection and exaltation, in this chapter. As we do so, we will call attention repeatedly to this bewildering phenomenon: When Jesus of Nazareth came 700 years later, and died on the cross, **these predictions were fulfilled with a literalness that astonishes, and an exactness that parallels mathematical certainty.**

(1) Messiah's Astonishing EXALTATION, Isaiah 52:13

"Behold, my servant shall prosper; He shall be exalted, and shall be extolled, and shall be raised very high" (Lit. trans., Isa. 52:13).

Before the depths of Messiah's humiliation is presented in

---

* Some unbelievers have sought to interpret this chapter as referring to "Suffering Israel," the nation, rather than to the "Suffering Messiah." But these five facts prove the theme of Isaiah 53 to be MESSIAH, not the Jewish people. (1) This prophecy speaks of an INDIVIDUAL all the way through. It is "HE shall grow up" (v. 2), "HE is despised . . . a MAN of sorrows" (v. 3), "HE was wounded" (v. 4), and so all through the chapter.

(2) Verse 8 is conclusive: the Sufferer was stricken for the transgressions of "My people" (Israel); and so He is an individual who suffers vicariously FOR the people; hence, He cannot be "the people."

(3) He is an INNOCENT Sufferer (vs. 7, 9), which could never be said of the nation Israel.

(4) He is a VOLUNTARY Sufferer, who willingly "pours out His soul unto death" (v. 12)—again depicting the death of an individual, not a nation. Moreover, Israel as a nation has never suffered willingly, voluntarily or vicariously.

(5) He is an UNRESISTING Sufferer, who "opened not His mouth" (v. 7), which could never be said of the nation Israel. Words could not make the meaning more clear to those open to truth; Isaiah 53 describes a sinless, voluntary, unresisting INDIVIDUAL who suffers vicariously for God's people Israel.

this section (Isa. 52:13—53:12), we are in the very beginning assured of His final VICTORY and GLORY. Franz Delitzsch calls attention to the progressive nature of the words "exalted . . . extolled . . . raised." He says,

"From these words we obtain this chain of thought: He will rise up, He will raise Himself still higher, He will stand on high."

And Stier rightly connects this with the three principal steps in the fulfillment of the prediction in Jesus of Nazareth after His death: Namely, His RESURRECTION, His ASCENSION, and His sitting down in EXALTATION at the RIGHT HAND OF GOD.

Here then we are at once confronted with Messiah's final end—to prepare us, as it were, for the shock of His temporary abasement: the "Servant of the Lord (after His sufferings) is seen rising from stage to stage; and at last He reaches an immeasurable height that towers above everything beside" (Delitzsch).*

The New Testament makes very clear the final exaltation of Christ after His sufferings and death:

"Who being the brightness of His glory, and the express image of His person, and upholding all things by the word of His power, when He had by Himself purged our sins"—by His atoning death on the cross—" (He) sat down on the RIGHT HAND OF THE MAJESTY ON HIGH" (Heb. 1:3).

"Christ Jesus, who being in the form of God, thought it not robbery to be equal with God: but . . . He humbled Himself, and became obedient unto death, even the death of the cross.

"WHEREFORE GOD ALSO HATH HIGHLY EXALTED HIM, and given Him a name which is above every name" (Phil. 2:6-11; see also Matt. 28:5, 6; Acts 1:3, 9; Eph. 1:20-23, etc.).

(2) Messiah's shocking ABUSE, Isaiah 52:14

"Just as many were astonished at Him, for so disfigured was He that His appearance was not human, and His form was not like that of the children of men" (Trans. by Delitzsch).

If Messiah's "exaltation" (v. 13) is astonishingly "high," His sufferings are even more astonishing. The word (shamem) here rendered "astonished" by the RV means "startled, confused, as it were petrified by paralyzing astonishment" (David Baron).

During the terrible hours before His crucifixion, the Lord

---

* Quoted in "The Servant of the Lord," p. 58.

Jesus was brutally manhandled, buffeted, scourged,* and abused in other ways. And on the cross, the crown of thorns, the nails driven through His quivering flesh, and the consequent agony of crucifixion in which every nerve, every muscle became "a flame of torture," added to the excruciating mental agony and soul suffering, so affected Him that His features became so marred and distorted that He no longer resembled a man. This horrifying fact is well nigh unbelievable, but it is clearly revealed of Messiah in the Old Testament, and just as clearly given in the records concerning the sufferings and death of Jesus the Christ in the New Testament.

"Pilate therefore took Jesus and scourged Him.* And the soldiers platted a crown of thorns and put it on His head** (John 19:1-2).

"Then they spit in His face, and buffeted (beat and manhandled Him); and others smote Him with the palms of their hands . . . and they stripped Him, and put on Him a scarlet robe. And when they had platted a crown of thorns, they put it upon His head . . . and mocked Him, and took the reed and smote Him on the head" (Matt. 26:67-68; 27:27-30).

God permitted, and Jesus endured, this horrible suffering not only to fulfill the prophetic picture, but to suffer in our stead. We ask—Who but the true Messiah **would want to be a Messiah like that?**

Before the cross, but leading up to it, His **face** was marred; on the cross, His **form** was marred, so the fulfillment of the prediction was complete. The bloody sweat, the traces of the crown of thorns, the spit on His face, and the result of the smiting on the head, disfigured His face; while the scourging, the buffeting, the nails driven through His hands and feet, the weight of the body, pulling it out of joint, and the final spear-thrust through His side, distorted His body. Add the extreme mental anguish and soul grief, and the result is, One so marred

---

* The scourging itself was violent, inhuman. The scourge was often made of leather thongs, fastened to a handle. At the ends of the thongs, at times, were fastened bits of sharpened metal or rock, that cut and lacerated the flesh of the victim, and turned the back into a bleeding pulp.

** We saw thorns in Bible lands having spines two to three inches long. When dried, they were very hard, pointed—and sharp as needles. Such a "crown" if pressed down on the brow, would puncture the skin in a score of places and cause both pain and a gory trickle of blood, which would result in matted, dishevelled hair, presenting a horrible appearance.

that He no longer resembled a man. How much He loved; how much He paid for our redemption!

As we humbly contemplate the intensity of the dreadful sufferings of the Saviour, may our hearts be "bowed with shame and sorrow for the sin which was the cause of it all, and may we have a greater love and undying gratitude to Him who bore all this for us" (David Baron).

(3) A Message that will STARTLE many Nations, Isaiah 52:15

"So shall He startle many nations; kings shall shut their mouths because of Him: for that which had not been told them shall they see; and that which they had not heard shall they understand" (Isa. 52:15).

God has devised a unique way to catch the attention, win the souls and win the devotion, of men. He Himself, in the Person of His Son, suffered so violently, creating so ghastly a scene, that it has IMPRESSED ALL AGES. The memory of Calvary startles the most dormant, pricks the most calloused, stirs the most lethargic. Men now understand both the love of God and the wisdom of God: CALVARY reveals it. Men see both the grace of God, and how God righteously can give righteousness to sinners who believe: For "Him who knew no sin He made to be sin on our behalf; that we might become the righteousness of God in Him" (2 Cor. 5:21). The Gospel will STARTLE many into believing.

(4) A Message that will be DISBELIEVED by Israel, Isaiah 53:1

"Who hath believed our report? and to whom is the arm of the Lord revealed?" (Isa. 53:1).

Strange as it may seem, though the shocking message of a Suffering Messiah will startle many nations, **yet it will find but few believers among Messiah's own people,** the Jews.

In the New Testament we read of the fulfillment of this prediction.

"But though He (Jesus) had done so many signs before them, yet they believed not on Him: that the word of Isaiah the prophet might be fulfilled, which he spake, Lord, who hath believed our report? And to whom hath the arm of the Lord been revealed?" (John 12:37-38).

(5) Messiah's Supernatural Birth and Spiritual Growth, Isaiah 53:2a

"For he shall grow up before Him as a tender plant, and as a root out of a dry ground" (Isa. 53:2a).

Messiah's supernatural birth is intimated in the phrase, "as a root out of a dry ground." A root growing out of dry ground is a miracle: one essential element (moisture) is missing. Messiah's birth was to be a miracle—the miracle of the virgin birth.

Note also this paradox: His supernatural, and yet natural, growth: "He shall **grow up**" (normally, much as other children), and yet it will be "before HIM," i. e., Messiah shall grow up **in Jehovah's Presence** and under His watchcare. Here too He will owe nothing to natural surroundings, for Messiah shall be "a tender plant . . . out of a dry ground." That is, Messiah will be a precious, wholesome plant in His youth, growing up before the Heavenly Father's watchful care, yet He will grow up in the midst of the universal spiritual dearth of the nation, in a desert of hardness, sin and unbelief. But it will be a normal process; He will "grow up." He will not "burst upon the world all at once, in a sudden splendour of daring and achievement: He will conform to God's slow, silent law of growth" (James Culross).

Isn't it amazing that God foretold the manner of His coming to earth, and the "growth" of His childhood, as well as the spirituality of His childhood? And, lo and behold, when Messiah came, all was fulfilled exactly as predicted. Messiah did NOT come as a full-grown king in His might, with dash and splendor; that is reserved for His **second** advent. In the New Testament, we read of the child Jesus:

"And the child grew, and waxed strong in spirit, filled with wisdom: and the grace of God was upon Him" (Luke 2:40).

(6) Messiah's Generation will fail to see and appreciate His Greatness, Isaiah 53:2:

"He hath no form nor comeliness; and when we shall see Him there is no beauty that we should desire Him" (v. 2).

When Messiah came, the people, looking for a mighty king and a political reformer, were disappointed in Him. Men did not see His beauty—the beauty of holiness—nor did they understand His mission. "He did not answer to the worldly ideal; having misread the prophecies, they found nothing to charm or attract them in 'Jehovah's Servant' when He came."

MESSIAH IN BOTH TESTAMENTS

The work of Messiah in His first advent, to make His soul an "offering for sin" was foreign to their ideas of what Messiah should be; Hence,

(7) He was DESPISED and REJECTED of Men, Isaiah 53:3

"He is despised and rejected of men: a man of sorrows, and acquainted with grief: and we hid as it were our faces from Him; He was despised, and we esteemed Him not" (v. 3). . . . . "We did esteem Him stricken, smitten of God, and afflicted" (v. 4).

"Rejected of men," says David Baron, "means actually 'rejected by men of high rank'." That is, He will have no men of high standing, no "important" men, few men of distinction, to support Him and His program with their authority and influence.

And so it proved to be in the life of Jesus the Christ. The following record from the New Testament reveals these facts:

The Pharisees (speaking to certain officers) said, "Are ye also deceived? Have any of the rulers or of the Pharisees believed on Him?" (John 7:47-48; see context).

Who but the infinite God, who knoweth the end from the beginning, would dare frame a prophecy like that, presenting Messiah as being **without** the support of the leaders of the people? **But history fully confirmed the truthfulness of the prediction.**

(8) Messiah will be known as a MAN OF SORROWS, Smitten of God, Afflicted, Isaiah 53:3,4

". . . a man of sorrows, and acquainted with grief: and we hid as it were our faces from Him; . . . we did esteem Him stricken, smitten of God, afflicted" (Isa. 53:3, 4).

The point here emphasized, and true in its fulfillment, is that Messiah will be "a man of pains" (Heb.)—sorrow of heart in all its forms.

Jesus' sorrow came, not only as He compassionately suffered with the ills of humanity, a sympathetic suffering, but also when He was repelled in His efforts to bless. His sorrow was overwhelming when the people rejected Him and continued in their lost estate. And this added to His sorrows, when men of rank and position turned from him—"hid their faces from Him." Instead of counting Him precious, "they esteemed Him not"—estimated Him "at nothing" (Luther).

"He came unto His own and His own received Him not" (John 1:11).

Worst of all, the people considered Him "smitten of God"— not realizing that He suffered to redeem **them,** and that He permitted Himself to be "made a curse" that He might save those He suffered for.

"Christ hath redeemed us from the curse of the law, being made a curse for us: for it is written, Cursed is every one that hangeth on a tree" (Gal. 3:13).

(9) Messiah's VICARIOUS SUFFERINGS

"Surely He hath borne OUR griefs and carried OUR sorrows" (v. 4); "He was wounded for OUR transgressions, He was bruised for OUR iniquities: the chastisement of OUR peace was upon HIM, and with HIS stripes (Heb., wounds) we are healed" (v. 5); "The Lord hath laid (Heb., caused to meet) on HIM the iniquity of us all" (v. 6); "For the transgression of my people was He stricken" (v. 8); "Thou shalt make His soul an offering for sin" (v. 10); "HE shall bear THEIR iniquities" (v. 11); "He bare the sin of many" (v. 12). (Quotations are from vs. 4, 5, 6, 8, 10, 11, 12).*

The outstanding fact of this chapter is the **vicarious, substitutionary sufferings of Messiah.** "Marvelous chapter," comments A. T. Pierson, "containing only twelve verses, yet fourteen times announcing the doctrine of the vicarious sacrifice for all human sin." The whole section (Isaiah 52:13—53:12) overflows with this conception, and never was the mystery solved until the Lord Jesus was "made sin for us" (2 Cor. 5:21) and "died for our sins" (1 Cor. 15:3).

Jehovah "hath caused to meet with overwhelming force in HIM the iniquity of us all" (Heb.). Messiah was the Divine Redeemer on whom fell "all the fiery rays of judgment which would have fallen on mankind" (Baron). How wonderful is God's grace through Christ's substitutionary atonement! So the cross became at once Christ's deepest humiliation, yet His highest glory—and the appointed means of bringing salvation to men.

When the Lord Jesus came, He fulfilled these Messianic predictions by His atoning death on the cross:

---

* "The Divine Author makes it impossible for any ingenuity or learning to eliminate the doctrine of vicarious atonement from this passage by presenting it so often, and in forms so varied and still the same, that he who succeeds in expelling it in one place is compelled to meet it in another" (Dr. Alexander).

"Who His own self bare our sins in His own body on the tree" (1 Peter 2:24).

(10) Messiah will suffer WILLINGLY and without Complaining, Isaiah 53:7

"He was oppressed, and He was afflicted, yet He opened not His mouth: He is brought as a lamb to the slaughter, and as a sheep before her shearers is dumb, so He openeth not His mouth" (v. 7).

Other sufferers usually register murmuring or complaining, especially when they are unjustly treated—but not so the suffering Messiah. He voluntarily submitted Himself to His appointed task of "bearing our sins" and went as a lamb to the slaughter. "In sublime and magnanimous silence Messiah will endure to the uttermost, because Jehovah wills it. . . . And here we look down into the unfathomed mystery of infinite love" (Culross).

In the New Testament, when Jesus the Christ was beaten, falsely accused, mistreated, mocked, spat upon, persecuted, manhandled, scourged, and crucified, there was no flame of resentment, no incriminations against His executioners, no loud complaining, but a prayer for His persecutors:

After many false witnesses appeared against Him, Jesus "held His peace." And the high priest wondered about it and said, "Answerest thou nothing?" (See Matt. 26:59-63).

And here is Jesus' prayer, while suffering the tortures of crucifixion: "Father forgive them for they know not what they do" (Luke 23:34).

This whole procedure is so unusual, so contrary to nature and human experience, one cannot help but be struck, startled, by both the strange prophecy and its even more remarkable fulfillment.

(11) When taken from Prison and Judgment, Messiah will have NO ADVOCATE to plead His Cause, no friend to declare His Innocence, Isaiah 53:8

"He was taken (Heb., snatched away, hurried away) from prison and from judgment: and who shall declare His generation?" (v. 8).

An alternate reading of the last phrase is, "And who (among) His generation shall declare (His innocence)?" The Sanhedrin had the custom in "trials for life" to call on those who knew anything in favor of the accused to come forward and declare it.* This was **not** observed in the trial of Jesus

---

* David Baron in "The Servant of Jehovah," p. 106.

of Nazareth, but rather, the proceedings at His hasty, mock, illegal trial before the Sanhedrin were in flagrant contradiction with their own regulations, and against all standards of right and fairness.

Jesus had to appear alone, and undefended, before the corrupt Jewish hierarchy and the representatives of the greatest Gentile power on earth at that time. **Not one person appeared to take His part.** Judas betrayed Him; Peter denied Him, with oaths; and the other disciples "forsook Him and fled" (Matt. 26:56). And many of the women that had during His ministry "ministered unto Him," stood "beholding (from) afar off" when He was crucified (Matt. 27:55). In the hour of His greatest need, humanly speaking, NOT ONE PERSON STOOD BY HIM. True, later on, after the weary hours of suffering had numbed His broken body, Mary His mother, a few faithful women, and John His beloved disciple, "stood by" at the cross; but during His trial and the early hours of His crucifixion He was left alone—absolutely alone. Never in the history of the world has anyone been so completely forsaken by friends and loved ones as Jesus was.

Jesus was arrested, NOT by proper officials, but by a mob, the rabble: "a great multitude with swords and staves, from the chief priests and elders of the people" (Matt. 26:47). Even Jesus commented on the inconsistency of their approach—"Are ye come out as against a thief with swords and staves for to take me? I sat daily with you teaching in the temple" . . . "but all this was done that the Scriptures of the prophets might be fulfilled" (Matt. 26:55, 56).

"False witnesses" were suborned to witness against Him "to put Him to death" (Matt. 26:59). And He was tried at night, which was illegal.

In the Roman court, when Pilate sought in vain for a cause to justly condemn Him, he asked the people, "What evil hath He done?" The only answers he got were the unreasonable shouts of the mob, edged on by their leaders, "let Him be crucified, let Him be crucified" (see Matt. 27:33). Then, when Pilate saw that words of reason and justice "prevailed nothing" and that a worse "tumult" was developing, he weakly washed his hands of the affair and turned Jesus over to them that they might crucify Him (see Matt. 27:24-26). This was the worst miscarriage of justice in the annals of all history.

But Christ's innocence was not only attested to by Pilate—"I find no fault in Him" (John 19:1)—but also by the Messianic prophet of old, "He had done no violence, neither was any deceit in His mouth" (Isa. 53:9).

(12) At the Moment of Death, Messiah's Humiliation was to end; and though Men planned His Burial "with the Wicked," Providence Planned It "with the Rich," Isaiah 53:9

"They (men) appointed Him His grave with the wicked (but) He was with a rich man after His death" (v. 9, Delitzsch).

"Dying as a criminal, ordinarily His body would have been flung over the wall to be burned like offal in the fires of Topheth (west of Jerusalem); but when His vicarious sufferings were finished no further indignity was permitted to His lifeless body" (A. T. Pierson). "And this remarkable coincidence," wrote Franz Delitzsch, is truly wonderful "if we reflect that the Jewish rulers would have given to Jesus the same dishonorable burial as that given to the two thieves, but the Roman authorities handed over His body to Joseph the Arimathean, a 'rich man' (Matt. 27:57) who placed it in his sepulchre in his own garden. And at once we see an agreement between the Gospel history and the prophetic words which could **only be the work of the God of both prophecy and its fulfillment,** inasmuch as no suspicion could possibly arise of there having been any human design of bringing the former into conformity with the latter."

The reason assigned for His honorable burial, which was so different from what had been planned or "appointed" for Him by His enemies, is, "He hath done no violence, neither was any deceit found in His mouth"—another reiteration of the absolute INNOCENCE of the Divine Sufferer.

Re-read with rapt interest the New Testament account of Jesus' burial, to find the perfect fulfillment:

"When the even was come, there came a rich man of Arimathea, named Joseph, who also himself was Jesus' disciple: He went to Pilate, and begged the body of Jesus. Then Pilate commanded the body to be delivered. And when Joseph had taken the body, he wrapped it in a clean linen cloth, and laid it in his own new tomb" (Matt. 27:57-60).

(13) After Messiah's Soul and Body have been made an Offering for Sin, God will "Prolong His Days," in RESURRECTION; and He will see His Seed, the Fruits of His Travail, Isaiah 53:10

"When thou shalt make his soul a trespass offering for sin, he shall see seed, he shall prolong his days, and the will of the Lord shall prosper in his hand" (Lit. trans., v. 10).

After Messiah's offering of Himself as a trespass offering, God will "prolong His days" in resurrection and He shall "see SEED"—saved souls—as the result of His sacrifice.

The fulfillment of this paradox, as we have already pointed out, is in the death and resurrection of Jesus the Christ, who

"Died for our sins according to the Scriptures . . . and rose again the third day, according to the Scriptures" (1 Cor. 15:3, 4).

This fact of Messiah's resurrection is in accord with other Old Testament Scriptures, such as Psalm 16:10:

"Thou wilt not leave my soul in Sheol; neither will Thou suffer Thine Holy One to see corruption."

Moreover, the will of God will "prosper" in Messiah's hand —Messiah will accomplish God's will with zeal, and He will indeed bring salvation and righteousness to both Israel and the nations (see Isa. 42:4).

The New Testament not only tells us of the glorious resurrection of Christ, but also of the beginning of His ministry after His resurrection—working through His disciples—by which multitudes were saved:

Acts 2:41: "Three thousand souls" were saved and added to the church.

Acts 4:4: "And the number (of men) who believed was about five thousand."

During the last nineteen centuries of church history, multiplied millions have believed on Christ and have been saved. Christ indeed has seen SEED, and the will of God is prospering in His hand. The gospel of Christ will eventually, after His second advent, come to final and complete triumph, and then "the earth shall be full of the knowledge of the Lord" as the waters now cover the sea (Isa. 11:9). Truly, the "Captain of our Salvation" is "bringing many sons unto glory" (Heb. 2:10).

(14) Not only will God be "Satisfied" with Messiah's Sacrifice, but through Knowing Messiah, many shall be JUSTIFIED, Isaiah 53:11

"He shall see the travail of his soul, and shall be satisfied; by His knowledge shall my righteous Servant make many righteous; for He shall bear their iniquities" (v. 11).

Here we are given a forecast of the tremendous truth, so fully developed by Paul in the New Testament, of JUSTIFI-

CATION BY FAITH, salvation by Grace—because Christ died for our sins and purchased a full redemption for all. This truth of justification by faith is the grand, central truth of the New Testament.

"Even the righteousness of God through faith in Jesus Christ, unto all them that believe . . . being justified freely by His grace through the redemption that is in Christ Jesus" (Rom. 3:22-24).

"For by grace are ye saved through faith" (Eph. 2:8-9). See also Romans 4:5-6; 5:15-19; Titus 3:5, etc.

Lest we forget that ALL grace bestowed upon believers is based on Messiah's sacrifice, we again are reminded that "He shall bear their iniquities." Dr. Alexander observes that there is an "antithesis here suggesting the idea of exchange or mutual substitution: **they** shall receive His righteousness, and **He** shall bear the heavy burden of their iniquities."

This of course is consonant with the doctrine of the New Testament:

"For He (God) hath made Him (Christ) to be sin for us, who knew no sin; that we (sinners) might be made the righteousness of God in Him" (2 Cor. 5:21).

(15) A Strange CIRCUMSTANCE of Messiah's Death is given, Isaiah 53:12

"He was numbered with the transgressors; and He bore the sin of many, and made intercession for the transgressors" (v. 12).

Similar to the mention of the disposition of Messiah's garments in Psalm 22, we here have a concomitant incident showing true DETAIL in prophecy, which marks it as genuine; for details in prophecy are the marks that immediately set it off as being of Divine origin—that is, if the fulfillment matches the prophecy.

The point here is, in this prophecy (v. 12), the word "transgressors" does not refer to ordinary sinners, but to "criminals" (Heb., **poshim**, criminals, open transgressors of the law of God and man). Furthermore, Delitzsch, Hengstenberg, Baron and others translate the reflexive verb used here: "He permitted Himself, voluntarily, to be numbered or 'reckoned' with criminals," showing again Messiah's willingness to suffer ALL that the Father had planned for Him.

It is of more than passing interest to recall that **Christ Him-**

self quoted this Scripture (Isa. 53:12) just before His own crucifixion:

"This that is written must yet be accomplished in Me, And He was reckoned among the transgressors" (Luke 23:37).

And so, as Delitzsch observed, this prediction and its fulfillment becomes "one of those remarkable coincidences which were brought about by Providence between the prophecies and our Saviour's passion," that Christ should have been crucified between two thieves (literally, "robbers"). See Luke 23:39-43.

Much has already been said about the vicarious nature of Messiah' sufferings as given in this chapter (Isaiah 53). In this the closing verse that fact again is stressed:

"He Himself bare the sin of many" (Lit. trans., v. 12).

Those familiar with the New Testament will recall many Scriptures that set forth the substitutionary nature of the death of Christ. We quote but two:

"Now once in the end of the age hath He (Christ) appeared to put away sin by the sacrifice of Himself. . . . So Christ was once offered to bear the sins of many" (Heb. 9:26, 28).

"For Christ also hath once suffered for sins, the just for the unjust, that He might bring us to God" (1 Pet. 3:18).

Many volumes have been written that show the wonders of Messianic prophecy in this chapter (Isaiah 53), and the fulfillment in the atoning death of Jesus the Christ as described in the New Testament. We believe, in touching the high spots as we have, and so calling attention again to these phenomena, these miracles in print, that the faith of many will either be generated or confirmed in both the supernatural character of the prophecies and their fulfillment. This shows clearly that Scripture has upon it "the stamp of its Divine Author—the mark of Heaven—the impress of eternity." Therefore, it is "beyond even the wildest credulity to believe that the resemblance in every feature and minutest detail between this prophetic portraiture in Isaiah 53, drawn centuries before His advent, and the account of His life, death and glorious resurrection, as narrated in the Gospels, can be mere accident or fortuitous coincidence" (David Baron).*

---

* In, The Servant of Jehovah, pp. vii, viii.

V. PROPHECIES DESCRIBING THE MESSIANIC OFFICES OF CHRIST

Christ, the Anointed One

Both the words "Christ" (Greek) and "Messiah" (Hebrew) mean the Anointed One.* Since the Fall of man, and consequent separation from God (Rom. 5:12), mankind has needed a Mediator, a Redeemer who can fill man's three basic needs:

(1) Sin left man guilty, lost, separated from God; hence, he needs forgiveness of sin, a restoration of a righteous character, and restoration to Divine fellowship. For this man needs a **Priest.** (2) Sin left man in spiritual darkness, ignorant of God; because of this, man needs a knowledge of the Word, Will and Ways of God: so, man needs a **Prophet.** (3) Sin, which is rebellion against God's government, left man with a rebellious nature that expresses itself also in antagonism to his fellowmen. Since man is a social creature, a unit in society, he needs authoritative governmental supervision. Hence, he needs a **King.** In Old Testament times, God provided these basic needs of mankind through His chosen prophets, priests and kings. But all human instruments come short and fail—so God planned from the beginning that He would provide the perfect Prophet, Priest and King for mankind in the perfect One, His only begotten Son.

In Old Testament times these three classes of public servants—prophets, priests and kings—were consecrated to office by an anointing with oil; prophets (see 1 Kings 19:16), priests (Lev. 8:12; Exod. 29:21), kings (1 Sam. 10:1; 16:12-13).

---

*For examples of the use of "anointed" in the Old Testament, see Lev. 4:3, 5; Ps. 2:2; Dan. 9:25, 26; 1 Sam. 2:10, etc. The word "anointed" occurs most frequently in Lev., 1 and 2 Samuel and in Psalms. The term "Messiah" (anointed) is applied to the high priest (Lev. 4:3, 5, 16; 6:22), who was a type-picture of Christ our High Priest. It occurs 18 times in 1 and 2 Samuel, but not always with Messianic connotation. It is found ten times in the book of Psalms, but again, not always with Messianic import. Ps. 2:2; 20:6; 28:8; 84:9; 89:51; 132:10,17 we believe are Messianic. Ps. 2:2 and Dan. 9:25, 26 are the outstanding passages that refer to the coming Messiah.

(1) CHRIST AS PROPHET

The Old Testament prophet represented God to the **nation,** and he gave His words, His message, to the people. When Messiah came, He would represent God perfectly and completely in **Person,** as well as in words, to Israel and to the world. When Jesus came He proved to be God's **perfect** Prophet:

"No man hath seen God at any time; the only begotten Son, which is in the bosom of the Father, he hath declared (revealed, manifested) Him" (John 1:18).

"He that hath seen Me hath seen the Father. . . . Believest thou not that I am in the Father, and the Father in Me? the words that I speak unto you I speak not of myself, but the Father that dwelleth in Me, He doeth the works" (John 14:9, 10).

As Prophet, the coming Messiah would be "like Moses":

"I will raise them up a Prophet from among their brethren, like unto thee (Moses), and will put my words in his mouth; and he shall speak unto them all that I have commanded him.

"And it shall come to pass, that whosoever will not hearken unto my words which He shall speak in my name, I will require it of him" (Deut. 18:15, 18, 19).

Moses was a remarkable character, and he was chosen, above all other prophets, to set forth in type the prophetic ministry of the coming Messiah. In these outstanding points, Christ was a Prophet "like unto Moses": Moses was a LAW-GIVER, a LEADER, a KING (Captain), a DELIVERER, a PROPHET (God's spokesman), and an INTERCESSOR for the people, with whom **God spake face to face;** so there arose not in Israel a prophet, like Moses (cf. Deut. 34:10-12; Numb. 12:6-8). He was the only man in Jewish history who exercised the functions of Prophet, Priest and King in one ministry.

How right the people were (John 6:14) who, when they had seen the miracle of Jesus' feeding the five thousand from a few loaves and fishes, said:

"This is of a truth that PROPHET that should come into the world." "That prophet" is also referred to in John 1:21.

Though Moses was great, Christ was infinitely greater. Moses as a "servant" was faithful; Christ as the "SON" was the perfect and omniscient PROPHET (cf. Heb. 3:5-6) who was ever faithful to Him who appointed Him" (Heb.3:2).

Peter summed up his sermon in the temple by these words:

"For Moses truly said unto the fathers, a prophet shall the Lord your God raise up unto you of your brethren, like unto me; Him shall ye hear in all things whatsoever He shall say unto you, and it shall come to pass that every soul which will not hear that Prophet shall be destroyed from among the people" (Acts 3:22-23).

Other references are made in both Testaments to the prophetic ministry of Christ. Both Isaiah 61:1 and Luke 4:18 refer to Christ's prophetic ministry, and both passages use the same words:

"The Spirit of the Lord is upon Me, because He hath anointed Me to preach the gospel to the poor; He hath sent Me to heal the broken-hearted, to preach deliverance to the captives," etc.

(2) CHRIST AS PRIEST

The Old Testament Priest, chosen by God, represented the people to God and offered sacrifices for their sins. He also had a ministry of compassion for the "ignorant and erring" (see Hebrews 5:1-4). This priesthood, of which Aaron was the first high priest, was imperfect, for the priests were sinners themselves and so they had first of all to offer sacrifice for their own sins, and then for the sins of the people (Heb. 5:3; 7:26; 9:7). Moreover, their priesthood was short-lived; it was frequently interrupted by death (Heb. 7:23). Furthermore, the offerings they offered were merely types, for "it is not possible that the blood of bulls and of goats should take away sins" (Heb. 10:4).

But in CHRIST, God's appointed High Priest, we have not only the perfect High Priest who liveth forever, but He gave HIMSELF for our sins, the perfect offering, the once-for-all, complete atonement for the sins of the race!

"For such an high priest became us, who is holy, harmless, undefiled, separate from sinners, and made higher than the heavens; who needeth not daily, as those high priests (of the old covenant), to offer up sacrifice, first for his own sins, and then for the people's: for this He did ONCE when He offered up HIMSELF.

"For the law maketh high priests which have infirmity; but the word of the oath, which was since the law, maketh the SON (our High Priest), who is consecrated for evermore" (Heb. 7:26-28). See also Heb. 9:11-14; 9:25-26).

So, by that one perfect Offering on the cross, Christ "perfected forever" them that are saved through faith in Him.

(See Heb. 10:10-14; 9:25-28; 7:23-28). Most of the book of Hebrews is devoted to the fact that in Christ Jesus God has given us His perfect HIGH PRIEST, who offered the perfect offering to atone for the sins of the race, and thereby give eternal life to all who accept Him as their Substitute and Saviour. Messiah gave both His body and His soul as an offering for sin and sinners (Isa. 53:5,10).*

Though the Aaronic priesthood presented to the people continuously their need of atonement for their sins, and that remission of sins could only be obtained through the shedding of blood (see Hebrews 9:22), the one person chosen to picture Messiah's ETERNAL priesthood was not Aaron, but Melchisedeck (see Heb. 5, 6, 7; Ps. 110:4). Melchisedeck as a type of Christ presents His eternal, unchanging priesthood (Heb. 7:3, "He abideth a priest continually.")

(3) CHRIST AS KING

"Yet have I set my king upon my holy hill of Zion" (Ps. 2:6).

Since man is not only an individual, but a social unit, he needs a KING (Government) to supervise his community life. So God, who first ruled the people of Israel through the patriarchs, later through "captains" (leaders, like Moses and Joshua), and later yet through "judges," finally consented

---

* In a sense, Messiah was anointed to be as a leper, when He bore the sins of the world. He was truly "made sin" for us (2 Cor. 5:21). Isaiah 53:4 intimates this. The AV reads, "We did esteem him stricken, smitten of God, afflicted." Jerome translates the first phrase, "We thought Him a leper." The word "stricken" was often used of the plague of leprosy; David Baron says of Isa. 53:4, " 'Stricken, smitten of God, afflicted' "— "every one of these three expressions was used of the plague of leprosy; and the phrases are intended to describe one suffering a terrible punishment for sin."

In Messiah's case it was for OUR sins, not His own, that He suffered so. Marvelous Grace, that Christ actually was willing to become as a LEPER for us!

In this connection, it is of more than passing interest to note that the leper who was to be "cleansed" in Old Testament times, was ANOINTED (Lev. 15:15-20). So, one might conclude that Christ, the Anointed of God, was not only anointed to be God's Prophet, Priest and King, but He also had an "anointing" to be the Sin-offering, and He literally became SIN ("the leprous One") for us. For such grace, such love, every believer will be eternally grateful.

to give them KINGS. In God's Messiah we have the perfect King—the "King of kings and the Lord of lords" who will have a wholly righteous, beneficent reign.

"Behold, the days come, saith the Lord, that I will raise unto David a righteous Branch, and a King shall reign and prosper, and shall execute judgment and justice in the earth. . . . and this is His name whereby He shall be called, THE LORD OUR RIGHTEOUSNESS" (Jerem. 23:5, 6).

"And the Spirit of the Lord shall rest upon Him (Messiah), and. . . with righteousness shall He judge . . ." (Isa. 11:2-5). See also Zech. 9:9; 1 Chron. 17:11-14; 2 Sam. 7:12-17; 23:1-8; Num. 24:17, etc.

God selected three great men to picture the work of Messiah as Prophet, Priest and King. Moses as prophet, Melchizedeck as priest, and David as king.

The term "Messiah" is found eighteen times in the book of Samuel, the book giving the life of David. Hannah, the mother of Samuel, has the honor of being the first one to use the word "Messiah" as referring to the Coming One; and it refers to Christ as God's anointed King.

"The Lord shall give strength unto His King, and exalt the horn of His anointed" (1 Sam. 2:10).

The coming of Messiah as King usually refers to His second advent, when He will establish His kingdom reign of righteousness. (See Isaiah 11:1-9; Micah 4:1-5, etc.).

Many Psalms speak of Messiah as the coming King. (See Psalm 2, Psalm 45, Psalm 47, Psalm 72, etc.).

In Psalm 2 we see the coronation of Messiah as King on Mount Zion (v. 6), and His inheritance of the heathen nations (v. 8).

In Psalm 45 we see the majesty and beauty of the King, and His glorious Bride.

In Psalm 47 we see Messiah as GOD, and His coronation as King of the earth (vs. 2,7).

Psalm 72 gives us the most complete picture in the book of Psalms of Messiah's coming kingdom and His reign of righteousness:

(1) Messiah is identified as the King's Son (v. 1)
(2) Messiah the King's Perfect Righteousness (vs. 2-4)
(3) Messiah the King's Wholesome Reign (vs. 5-7)
(4) Messiah the King's Universal Dominion (vs. 8-11)
(5) Messiah the King's Divine Compassion (vs. 12-14)

(6) Messiah the King's Reign produces Material and Spiritual Prosperity (vs. 15-17)

(7) Perfect Praise of the Lord God during Messiah the King's Reign (vs. 18-19)*

The New Testament Witness that Jesus is the Christ, the Anointed of God

In the New Testament, Jesus the Christ is clearly set forth as God's anointed Prophet (John 17:8) who gives His people God's words, God's anointed Priest, who "through the eternal Spirit offered Himself without spot to God, to purge your conscience . . . . " (Heb. 9:14), and as God's coming "King of kings and Lord of lords" (Rev. 19:16).

In Hebrews 1:9 Christ is seen as the anointed of God:

"Thou hast loved righteousness and hated iniquity, therefore God, even thy God, hath ANOINTED thee with the oil of gladness above thy fellows."

We have referred before to Luke 4:18 where Christ said He was the One "anointed to preach the gospel to the poor" that Isaiah had spoken about (Isa. 61:1).

In Revelation 1:5 Jesus is presented as Prophet, Priest and King:

---

* Messiah is also presented as the Priest-King: "A Priest on His throne." The message to Joshua in Zechariah 6:13 certainly looks beyond Joshua to the Messiah, for there are statements in the passage that can be fulfilled only in One greater than man.

"Thus speaketh the Lord of hosts, saying, Behold the man whose name is the Branch"—so identifying the message definitely as being Messianic —"He shall grow out of His place"—having a natural yet supernatural growth as a child (cf. Isa. 53:2)—"and He shall build the temple of the Lord"—which Christ is doing even now (Eph. 2:21,22)—"and He shall bear the glory"—the glory as of the only begotten of the Father, full of grace and truth (John 1:14)—"and shall sit and rule upon His throne"— as King and Priest, even as Melchisedeck (Ps. 110:4, 2)—"and the counsel of peace shall be between them both"—as King Messiah will bring peace (Ps. 72:7; Ps. 46:9), and as Priest He will bring peace through the blood of His cross (Col. 1:20; Eph. 1:7).

In Jeremiah 30:21 is another remarkable Messianic passage, giving a similar testimony. Messiah will be the King-Priest: He will "rule" the people, and He will "draw near and approach unto God" as the perfect MEDIATOR (cf. 1 Tim. 2:5).

Turning to the New Testament we see that the "Lion of the Tribe of Judah, the root of David" (Rev. 5:5)—Christ as King—is also the One who hath "an unchangeable priesthood" (Heb. 7:24-28).

"And from Jesus Christ who is the faithful witness (Prophet), and the first begotten of the dead, and the prince of the kings of the earth (King). Unto Him that loved us, and washed us from our sins in His own blood (Priest)."

And also in Hebrews 1:1-3 Christ is presented as Prophet, Priest and King:

"God . . . . hath in these last days spoken unto us in His Son (Prophet) . . . who, when He had by Himself purged our sins (Priest), sat down (as King) on the right hand of the Majesty on high."

"BEHOLD" . . . "GOD'S BRANCH"

Other Bible teachers have called attention to the remarkable fourfold use of the Messianic name **"the BRANCH"** in the Old Testament, and the frequent use of "Behold," in connection with God's Messiah, the Branch. "Behold" is used as God's **"Ecce Homo"** in the Old Testament. Taken together (the "Beholds" with "the Branch") they present a beautiful summary of the CHRIST of the four Gospels. Here is the fourfold use of "the Branch" and "Behold" as used of Messiah in the Old Testament.

(1) As **KING**

"Behold the days come, saith the LORD, that I will raise unto David a righteous BRANCH, and a KING shall reign and prosper" (Jerem. 23:5, 6).
"BEHOLD—thy KING cometh" (Zech. 9:9).
This corresponds to the Gospel of MATTHEW, where Christ is presented as KING.

(2) As **SERVANT OF THE LORD**

"BEHOLD, 1 will bring forth My Servant the BRANCH" (Zech. 3:8).
This corresponds to the Gospel of MARK, where Christ is presented as the SERVANT OF THE LORD.

(3) As **SON OF MAN**

"Thus speaketh the Lord of hosts, saying, BEHOLD the MAN whose name is the BRANCH" (Zech. 6:12,13).
This corresponds to the Gospel of LUKE, where Christ is presented as the ideal and the representative MAN.

(4) As the **SON OF GOD**

"BEHOLD your God" (Isa. 40:9).
"In that day shall the BRANCH of the LORD be beautiful and glorious" (Isa. 4:2).
This corresponds to the Gospel of JOHN, where Christ is presented as the SON OF GOD—yes, GOD HIMSELF in the flesh.

These four uses of "the BRANCH" are the only four instances in the Hebrew Sscriptures (except Jerem. 33:15, which is a repetition of the thought in Jerem. 23:5, 6) where Messiah is designated by the title "The Branch." Several times Messiah is introduced in the Old Testament by the word "Behold"—as though to call special attention to HIM.*

OTHER NAMES OF MESSIAH IN THE OLD TESTAMENT

There are scores of names of Messiah in the Old Testament; we mention but a few.

"The Servant of the Lord"

In Isaiah, Messiah is frequently called "The Servant of the Lord," or, "My Servant." (See Isa. 42:1; 52:13, etc.). As the "Servant of the Lord (Jehovah)" He is the exponent of righteousness and true humility, the teacher and Redeemer of mankind. He fufills all God's desires: hence, He is:

The Second Adam—the Perfect Man
The Second Israel—the Perfect Servant
The Second Moses—the Perfect Prophet
The Second David—the Perfect King
The Second High Priest—the Perfect Priest

The growing purposes of God toward the whole human race, which were manifested in the creation of Adam, the election of Israel, the raising up of Moses, the appointment of Aaron, and the call of David are "brought to their full completion by, in and through Christ" (Delitzsch).

The "Shepherd"

Isaiah sees Messiah as "the Servant of the Lord"; Ezekiel

---

* Professor Godet says, "Just as a gifted painter, who wished to immortalize for a family the complete likeness of the illustrious father, would avoid any attempt in combining in a single portrait the insignia of all the various offices he had filled by representing him in the same picture as general and magistrate, as a man of science and as a father of a family; but would prefer to paint four distinct portraits. So the Holy Spirit, to preserve for mankind the perfect likeness of Him who was its chosen representative, God in man, used means to impress upon the minds of the writers of the Gospels, four different images."

ALL of these four accounts of the life of Christ present Him as the MESSIAH—God's perfect Prophet, Priest, King and Son of God—yet each has a different emphasis. In Matthew He is KING; in Mark He is the SERVANT OF JEHOVAH; in Luke He is the SON OF MAN; and in John He is the SON OF GOD.

sees Him as "the Shepherd of Israel" (see Ezekiel 34:23 and 37:24, where "David" is used as a name of Messiah. "David" means "beloved").

Christ, the truly Beloved of the Father, took both the name and the character of the true Shepherd. (See John 10).

More Names and Titles of Messiah

Messiah is frequently called "the Angel of the Lord"—the Messenger of the Lord. (See Judges 2:1; 6:12-13, 21-22). He is also "the Stone" or "the Rock" (Isa. 8:14); "the Corner" (Isa. 28:16); "Nail" (Isa. 22:21-25); "Battle Bow" (Zech. 10:4); "Shiloh" (Gen. 49:10); "Star" (Numb. 24:17), etc.

The Name "JESUS" in the Old Testament

In an enlightening study: "YESHUA IN THE TENACH" (The Name JESUS in the Old Testament), Arthur E. Glass points out the amazing fact that the name JESUS is actually hidden in the Old Testament, and "is found about one hundred times from Genesis to Habakkuk." "Every time the Old Testament uses the word SALVATION (especially with the Hebrew suffix meaning 'my' 'thy,' or 'His,' with very few exceptions (when the word is used in an impersonal sense) it is identically the same word as YESHUA (Jesus) used in Matthew 1:21," says Mr. Glass. He continues: "This is actually what the angel said to Joseph:

" 'And she shall bring forth a son, and thou shalt call His name YESHUA (SALVATION), for He shall save His people from their sins.' "

Let us see how it works out in a few Old Testament passages. In Psalm 9:14 David says, "I will rejoice in thy salvation." What he actually said was, "I will rejoice in thy YESHUA (Jesus)." And in Isaiah 12:2, 3, we have something truly wonderful. SALVATION is mentioned three times, presenting three great facets of Jesus and His Salvation. We give them (quoting Glass) as they read in the Hebrew, with Jesus as the embodiment and the personification of the word Salvation:

"Behold, mighty One (or God the Mighty One) is my YESHUA (a reference to Jesus in His pre-incarnation, eternal existence, cf. John 1:1); I will trust and not be afraid; for JAH-JEHOVAH is my strength and my song: He also is become my YESHUA (Jesus, the Word made flesh; John 1:14). Therefore, with joy shall ye draw water out of the wells of YESHUA (Jesus crucified, waters of salvation flowing from Calvary, cf. John 7:37-39).

VI. THE DEITY OF MESSIAH (CHRIST) IN BOTH TESTAMENTS

The Dual Nature of Messiah

For a correct comprehension of the Person of Messiah, it is necessary to understand that He has a DUAL NATURE, but is a single personality: He is very God and perfect man; rather, He is the God-man, God and man in one, indivisible personality. His humanity is seen in such names and titles as Son of man, Son of David, Son of Abraham, etc. His Deity is seen in such names and titles as Son of God, God, Lord, Jehovah, El, Elohim, etc. The purpose of this present study is to present this fact of supreme importance: the Bible reveals Messiah (Christ) to be GOD MANIFEST IN THE FLESH.

The Deity of Christ as Presented in Hebrews, Chapter 1

In the first six verses of Hebrews 1, these ten facts are presented about Christ, **all of which prove and establish the fact of His Deity;** for none of thes facts could be postulated about a mere man.

(1) Christ (Messiah) is called God's "SON" in contrast to the "prophets" who were only men, even though they were inspired men, vs. 1-2: "God, who . . . spake in time past unto the fathers **by the prophets,** hath in these last days spoken unto us in His Son."

(2) Christ is "Heir of all things," v. 2. He is the Son, therefore He is the heir.

(3) The worlds (universe) "were made through Him (Christ)," v. 2. This not only proves His pre-existence, but reveals Him as the active agent in creation. Cf. John 1:1-3: "all things were made by Him (Christ); **and without Him was not anything made that was made" (v. 3).**

(4) He is identified with the GLORY of God as much as the brightness of the sun is identified with the sun: "who being the effulgence (brightness) of His Person, " v. 3.

(5) He is identified with the CHARACTER of God as much as the impress of a seal exactly reproduces the seal: "the very image (impress) of His Person," v. 3.

(6) He (Messiah, Christ) is the One who upholds this vast, well-nigh infinite Universe, which of course is the work of an omnipotent God: upholding all things by the word of His power," v. 3. Cf. Colossians 1:16, 17: "For by Him (Christ) were all things created. . . and by Him all things consist (Gr., are held together)."

(7) He, Christ, accomplished the redemption of the race ALONE. No sinful man, not even a perfect man, could redeem a race of billions of lost sinners. It takes an infinite Sacrifice to atone for a world of

sinners. "When He had BY HIMSELF purged (made purification of) our sins," v. 3.

(8) He now occupies the highest position in the Universe next to the Father: at God's right hand, sharing with God the Father the Eternal Throne: "He sat down on the right hand of the Majesty on high," v. 3. That Christ, the Lamb of God, shares the Eternal Throne is evident from Rev. 22:1: "the Throne (singular) of God and of the Lamb."

(9) He is "much better" than the angels, v. 4: "having become by so much better than the angels." (RV).

(10) Again, the Father-Son relationship of the Father and Messiah is established. Even the angels are commanded to worship Him (Messiah); see v. 6: "Let all the angels of God worship Him." Remember, only GOD is to be worshipped (Matt. 4:10). "Thou art My Son"—the Father's testimony to the Son, v. 5. Cf., v. 5, l.p.: "I will be to Him a Father, and He shall be to Me a Son."

In the rest of the first chapter of Hebrews (together with the Old Testament Scriptures from which citations are made in this first chapter of Hebrews), we discover this impressive fact: Messiah is called by the three primary names and titles of God used in the Old Testament, and by the two primary names of Deity used in the New Testament.

In verse 8, God the Father, speaking to God the Son (Messiah) calls Him GOD (Gr., Theos). This eighth verse is a quotation from Psalm 45:6, where the primary name of God, Elohim, is used of Messiah: "Thy throne, O God (Heb., Elohim), is forever and ever."

In Hebrews 1:10, God the Father, still speaking to and about the SON (Messiah) calls Him LORD (Gr., Kurios). This is a quotation from Psalm 102:25-27. These verses (Ps. 102:25-27) refer to JEHOVAH; see Ps. 102:16, 19, 21, 22. Let us now quote this passage from the New Testament:

"And Thou Lord (Gr., Kurios), in the beginning hast laid the foundation of the earth; and the heavens are the works of Thine hands: they shall perish: but Thou remainest: and they shall all wax old as doth a garment; and as a vesture shall they fold up, and they shall be changed: but Thou art the same, and Thy years shall not fail" (Heb. 1:10-12).

Notice that in these verses (Heb. 1:10-12):

(1) The Father (as in verse 8) is still speaking to the Son.

(2) The Father says that the Son is the Creator of the Universe: "the heavens are the works of Thine hands" (v. 10).

(3) The Father says of the Son that He is ETERNAL—UNCHANGEABLE. The Universe will get old as a used garment, but of the SON (Messiah) He says, "Thy years shall not fail" (v. 12).

The writer of the book of Hebrews adds two more inspired comments concerning Messiah:

(1) "But to which of the angels said He (God the Father) at any time, Sit on My right hand until I make thine enemies thy footstool?" (v. 13) —again showing the exalted position of Messiah: at God's right hand.

(2) "Until I make thine enemies thy footstool" (v. 13)—assuring all of Messiah's ETERNAL VICTORY.

Since God the Father has testified so emphatically in this chapter of the Deity of Christ, and has given us 15 statements that fully set forth the DEITY OF MESSIAH, it is folly for any one to deny that basic truth. In fact, our eternal salvation depends on our accepting this truth of Christ's Deity:

"If ye believe NOT that I am He (the Lord Jehovah), ye shall die in your sins"* (John 8:24).

Old Testament Statements about the Deity of Messiah

Turning to Old Testament predictions and comparing them with their New Testament fulfillments, we discover:

(1) Jehovah calls Messiah His "Fellow" (equal):

"Awake, O sword, against my Shepherd, and against the man that is My Fellow, saith the Lord of hosts" (Zech. 13:7).

In the New Testament Christ said the same thing: "I and My Father are one" (John 10:30).

Paul, inspired by the Holy Spirit, testifies in Philippians 2:6 that Christ is "equal with God." "Christ Jesus who, being in the form of God, thought it not robbery (a thing to be grasped after) to be EQUAL WITH GOD."

(2) In Isaiah 9:6 we have a forecast of Messiah's humanity, Deity, and Kingship

Names of Deity are given to the coming Messiah that none but the wilfully unbelieving can mistake:

"For unto us a child is born (Messiah's humanity), unto us a Son is given (His eternal Sonship, in the Trinity) . . . and His name shall be called Wonderful, Counsellor, THE MIGHTY GOD (Heb., El Gibor), THE FATHER OF ETERNITY—both names of Deity—"the Prince of Peace."

Remember, names as used in Hebrew express that which a person IS; being called anything means being that thing. So, when Messiah is called by the name "THE MIGHTY GOD" it means He IS the Mighty God.

(3) Messiah is called GOD (El, ELOHIM) in the Old Testament

---

* Christ here uses the words "I AM" which is the meaning of the name Jehovah (see Exodus 3:14), so identifying Himself as the JEHOVAH of the Old Testament.

The following Scriptures show that Messiah is called GOD (Heb., **El, Elohim**):

"Say unto the cities of Judah, Behold your God (Elohim). Behold, the Lord GOD (Elohim) will come with strong hand" (Isa. 40:9, 10).

We already have referred to Psalm 45:6 where Messiah is called GOD: "Thy throne, O GOD, is forever and ever."

In Psalm 47:7, 8 we read of Messiah's second advent: "For GOD (Elohim) is King over the whole earth" . . . "GOD (Elohim) reigneth over the nations." It is abundantly clear that it will be Messiah (Christ) who will reign over the nations. See Rev. 11:15; 19:16; 1 Cor. 15:24, 25.

(4) Messiah is also called JEHOVAH in the Old Testament

In Zechariah 2:10 we read that the Lord (Jehovah) has said: "Lo, I come, and I WILL DWELL IN THE MIDST OF THEE."

"For the LORD (JEHOVAH) most high . . . is a great King over all the earth" (Ps. 47:2). (The context shows this is a Messianic Psalm, looking forward to the second advent of Christ).

In Jeremiah 23:5-6 we read that Messiah shall be called JEHOVAH OUR RIGHTEOUSNESS."

In Psalm 102:16 we are told that: "The LORD (JEHOVAH) . . . hath appeared in His glory."

In Zechariah 14:9 we read that it is "the LORD (JEHOVAH)" who "shall be King over all the earth." And to prove that it is JEHOVAH IN THE FLESH who is King, we see in verses three and four of the same chapter that "Jehovah shall go forth . . . and His feet shall stand in that day upon the mount of Olives."

In Zechariah 12:10 there can be no mistaking of the meaning: "They shall look upon Me (Jehovah) WHOM THEY HAVE PIERCED"—a reference of course to the crucified Messiah.

In a crystal clear prediction in Isaiah 40:3, Messiah is called both Jehovah (LORD) and (Elohim (GOD): "The voice of him that crieth in the wilderness, Prepare ye the way of the LORD (Jehovah), make straight in the desert a highway for our God (Elohim)."

In the New Testament this Scripture is quoted, showing its fulfillment in Christ and in John the Baptist, His forerunner (see Matt. 3:1-3).

In both Zephaniah 3:14-15 and Isaiah 12:6 we learn that it is Jehovah Himself the "Holy One" of Israel who will be in their midst: "The King, even JEHOVAH, is in the midst of thee" (Zeph. 3:14, 15).

That JEHOVAH OF HOSTS is a title of Messiah, we see clearly by comparing Isaiah 6:1-3 with John 12:41; and Isaiah 8:13, 14 with 1 Peter 2:5-8.

(5) Jesus in the New Testament claimed to be the great "I AM" of the Old Testament

Jehovah says of Himself in Isaiah 43:10:

"Ye are My witnesses, saith Jehovah, and My servant whom I have chosen: that ye may know and believe Me, and understand that I AM HE."

It is therefore full of significance that Christ in the New Testament made the same claim in John 8:24; 13:19; 4:26; Mark 13:6, etc. "That ye may believe that I AM HE" (John 13:19). Jesus frequently used the expression "I AM" in connection with some special revelation of His Person or work:

"I AM the Good Shepherd" (John 10:14)
"I AM the Door" (John 10:9)
"I AM the Light of the World" (John 8:12)
"I AM the Way, the Truth and the Life" (John 14:6)

(6) The Title of God, Adonai, is given to Messiah in the Old Testament:

"Behold, I will send My messenger, and he shall prepare the way before Me: and the Lord (Heb., **Adonai**) whom ye seek shall suddenly come to His temple" (Mal. 3:1).

The "messenger" who prepared the way for the coming of the Lord (Adonai) was John the Baptist; and the Lord for whom he prepared the way was Messiah—Jesus of Nazareth.

"The LORD (Jehovah) said unto my Lord (Adonai), Sit Thou at My right hand, until I make thine enemies thy footstool" (Ps. 110:1).

On the Day of Pentecost, Peter quoted this passage in his sermon to prove both the Messiahship and the Deity of Christ of Nazareth. See Acts 2:34-36; cf. Matt. 22:41-45, where Jesus Himself proves to the Pharisees that Messiah is not only the son of David, He is also his Lord (Adonai).

(7) The Old Testament also teaches the PRE-EXISTENCE OF MESSIAH

In Psalm 72:17 we read in the English translation:

"His name shall continue as long as the sun."

But the original Hebrew reads:

"Before the sun was, His name (was) Yinon." This is the only occurrence in Scripture of the word "Yinon," and all ancient Jewish commentators agree that it is a name of Messiah.

In Proverbs 8:22-24 we read of the Pre-existence of Messiah:

"The LORD possessed me in the beginning of His way, before His works of old. I was set up from everlasting, from the beginning, or ever the earth was." That this description of "Wisdom," personified, is really a description of the Eternal Messiah, is beyond doubt.

The New Testament also teaches the pre-existence of Christ, the Eternal Word:

"In the beginning WAS the Word and the Word was with God, and the Word was God. The same was in the beginning with God" (John 1:1-2).

(8) The Old Testament presents Messiah as "the GLORY OF THE LORD"—a Phrase signifying Deity

"And the Glory of the LORD shall be revealed, and all flesh shall see it." (Isa. 40:5; cf. Isa. 40:3-4, which proves this verse, 5, to be Messianic).
In the New Testament, we read of Messiah's Incarnation:
"And the Word was made flesh, and dwelt among us (and we beheld His glory, the GLORY AS OF THE ONLY BEGOTTEN OF THE FATHER), full of grace and truth" (John 1:14).

The Deity of Christ taught in the New Testament

We have before shown from Hebrews 1, that the New Testament fully teaches the Deity of Christ (Messiah). This teaching of the Deity of Christ pervades the entire New Testament, and can be seen in scores of direct statements and hundreds of inferences. Some of the inferences of Christ's Deity are drawn from:

(1) His power to forgive sin (see Mark 2:10).
(2) His right to receive worship (Matt. 2:11; 8:2; 9:18; 14:33, etc.).
(3) His supernatural powers (see all His miracles, as recorded in the Gospels, e.g., Mark 2:11; 3:5, 10, 11; etc.
(4) His sinless character (Heb. 7:26; 1 Pet. 2:22; 1 John 3:5; cf. Luke 18:19, where our Lord taught, indirectly, that none should call Him good unles they admit He is God, for there is "none good but God.")
(5) His atoning death proves His deity—for none but GOD could atone for the race (Heb. 2:9).
(6) His bodily resurrection proves His deity (Rom. 1:4).
(7) The many promises He gave that demand Deity to fulfill: such as Matthew 11:28, 29; Matt. 28:19, 20; John 14:23.
(8) Men are to trust Him even as they do the Father (John 14:1-3).
(9) He is the Creator and Sustainer of the Universe (John 1:1-3; Colossians 1:16, 17).
(10) He has all the Characteristics of Deity: Omnipresence, Omniscience, Omnipotence, etc. (See Matt. 28:20; John 14:23; John 3:13; John 16:30; Matt. 28:18; etc.

Some direct statements of Christ's Deity:

John 1:1-3: "the Word was God."
Note the striking testimony to Christ's Deity in Luke 1:68 and 1:76.
See also Romans 9:5; John 20:28; Col. 1:14, 17; 1 Cor. 2:8; 1 Tim. 6:14-16; Titus 2:13, Hebrews, chapter 1, etc.

THE TRINITY

That Messiah should be both GOD and yet be sent by God, is a mystery unravelled in the teaching of the Trinity. God is One God, existing in Three Persons: Father, Son (Messiah) and Holy Spirit.

"The Father sent the Son to be the Saviour of the world" (1 John 4:14).

It is not our present purpose to expound the Scriptures on the teaching of the Trinity, but we give here some references which directly teach, or intimate, the Trinity. Note the following:

(1) In Genesis 1:1 the word "God" (**Elohim**) is in the plural, and it is followed by a verb (created) which is in the singular—thus intimating a plurality of Persons in the Godhead who are as ONE.

(2) In Deuteronomy 6:4 the word for "one" (God) is **"achad"** which is the word for a compound unity, not an absolute unity. It (achad) is used in Gen. 2:24: Adam and Eve (a man and his wife) shall be one (achad) flesh—two persons as "one." See also Gen. 11:5; Numb. 13:23; Jud. 20:1,2.

(3) There are many direct statements of the Trinity in the Old Testament, as Isa. 48:16; 48:17; 11:2; 42:1; 61:1; 63:7-10; Zech. 2:10,11; Num. 6:24-27 (note the singular "My name" in verse 27 that follows the threefold use of the name LORD in vs. 24-26).

(4) Many Scriptures intimate the Trinity, as in Gen. 1:26,27 where God says "Let US" (implying more than one Person in the Godhead); see also Gen. 11:5-7; Isa. 6:8; Gen. 3:22.

(5) The Trinity is clearly taught in the New Testament: see Matthew 28:19, 20; Matt. 3:16, 17; John 14:16; Eph. 4:4-6; 2 Cor. 13:14; Heb. 9:14; Rev. 1:4-5. See (in Tregelles' Greek text) a most remarkable triple reference to the Trinity in Revelation 1:8:

"I—(1) I AM (2) the Alpha and the Omega, (3) the Beginning and the ending, saith (1) the Lord (**Kurios**), (2) God (**Theos**) . . . (3) the Almighty (**Pantokrator**), (1) the One being, (2) and the One who was, and (3) the One who is coming.

VII. TYPES AND INDIRECT FORECASTS OF MESSIAH

The Bible is unique in its TYPE-PICTURES of the coming Messiah as well as in its distinct and definite prophecies.*

A "type" may be defined as a divinely created illustration

---

* The Bible is unique, without parallel— without even a serious competitor—in at least seven features: (1) It alone, of all books in the world, has genuine prophecy. (2) The Bible alone contains an intricate system of "types" in the Old Testament, fufilled in the New Testament, as shown in this chapter. (3) The Bible alone contains the record of genuine, credible miracles, fully attested by adequate witnesses. (4) Of all books in the world, the Bible alone presents the Perfect Character (the Messiah). (5) The Bible alone, of all national history books, portrays its characters without bias, and presents them as they are, their weaknesses and failures as well as their strong points. (6) The Bible alone, of all ancient books, is consonant with all the facts of nature and true scientific discoveries that it refers to, even though it was written ages before the modern scientific era. (7) Though written by nearly 40 human authors, the Bible has a phenomenal UNITY that shows the superintendence of its Divine Author.

of spiritual truth. A person, place, thing, event, or a series of events, by divine foresight and planning, becomes an object lesson, a PICTURE—with correspondence of details—of its anti-type (fufillment). God and Christ, Satan and Antichrist, believers and unbelievers, the yielded Christian life and the world, are the subjects of Biblical types. "Even where no direct prediction is found," comments A. T. Pierson, "indirect forecasts (through types) referring to Christ may be distinctly traced "all through the Bible." How true! Types of Christ—prophetic pictures giving indirect forecasts—abound in the Old Testament. We could write a book of several hundred pages and barely skirt the edges of the vast field of Biblical types. In our limited space, we can but suggest some of the marvels of this field of Biblical research and study.

The Cross of Christ has perhaps more foreshadowings, more types that preview and prefigure the sacrifice of the Son of God, than any other thing in the Bible. Every Passover lamb slain (with its attendant ceremonies of the sprinkling of the blood of the lamb on the door posts, the eating of the roasted lamb, etc.—see Exodus 12:1-13);* every Levitical offering brought to the altar and sacrificed (see Leviticus, chapters 1-6); and every other blood offering presented, "from the hour of Abel's altar-fire down to the last passover of the passion week, pointed as with flaming finger to Calvary's Cross!" . . . And there we see "the convergence of a thousand lines of prophecy (indirect forecasts) . . . as in one burning focal point of dazzling glory" (A. T. Pierson).

Turn where you will, you find pictures of CHRIST in the Old Testament.

In Genesis (especially rich in prophetic forecasts of Christ) you find ADAM presented as the Head of God's creation—a type of Christ as Head of the new creation (see 1 Cor. 15:45-49). The ARK was the only means of saving people from the judgment of the Flood (Gen. 6-9); Christ is the "Ark

---

* When the Passover lamb was roasted "a spit was thrust lengthwise through its body, and another transversely from shoulder to shoulder; every passover lamb was thus transfixed on a cross. In like manner, when Moses lifted up the brazen serpent (Num. 21) it was not on a pole but on a banner staff— i.e., a cross" (A. T. Pierson, in "Many Infallible Proofs," p. 204).

of Salvation"; all who by faith come to Him are saved from the coming flood of God's judgment against sin. The Offering of Issac is an especially rich type (Gen. 22) of the offering up of Jesus, by His Father. The life of Joseph——beloved of his father, but hated and rejected by his brethren (Gen. 37)—is an amazing picture, with over 100 corresponding features, of the Lord Jesus Christ, who likewise was beloved of His Father but hated and rejected by His brethren. Joseph was sent to the Gentiles, where he obtained a bride, and was the means of feeding multitudes and saving them from destruction (Gen. 39-47); so Christ, rejected by His brethren (the Jews) has been preached to the Gentiles—and vast multitudes have been preserved and fed the Bread of Life by Him. Joseph finally reveals himself to his brethren—and becomes the means of preserving them too. So Christ, in the latter days, will reveal Himself to Israel and save many of them (see Zech. 12:10; Rom. 11:25, 26).

In Exodus, we see not only the PASSOVER LAMB (already referred to, Exodus 12), but the life and ministry of MOSES, as an outstanding type of Christ. Moses, a Shepherd in his youth, and at first rejected by his brethren, flees to a Gentile country, where he gets a Gentile bride; later, when he returns to liberate Israel he is accepted as their leader, and leads them out of the house of bondage (Egypt) with great victory. This type of Christ is thrilling: for it speaks of Christ's rejection at His first coming to Israel and His eventual acceptance and leadership over Israel. (See Acts 7:22-37, especially v. 35).

The life of DAVID in First and Second Samuel, is a similar picture of the Messiah. David was a shepherd in his youth; at first he was rejected by Saul, who sought to kill him; later, David was accepted by the nation, anointed, and crowned as their king. And so he becomes a TYPE of the Greater David who was at first the "Good Shepherd" who gave His life for His sheep; later on He will reign as KING.

Aaron and Melchisedeck picture Christ as HIGH PRIEST; Moses and Samuel (and the rest of the prophets) adumbrate Christ as the great Prophet.

Christ explained the BRAZEN SERPENT, uplifted before the people as a means of deliverance from the judgment of death that fell on them because of their sin (see Numbers 21:5-9), as a TYPE OF HIS WORK OF REDEMPTION AND SALVATION THROUGH HIS CROSS (see John 3:14-18).

JONAH, swallowed by the whale, passing through an experience of "death and resurrection," and then preaching to the Gentiles, is a picture of the One who was "three days and three nights" in the heart of the earth, and who came forth —as Jonah did—in resurrection. (See Matt. 12:40, where Christ Himself makes Jonah's experience a type of His own, in death and resurrection).

The TABERNACLE (Exod. 25-31; 35-40), is one of the most extensive and meaningful of all the types. Its priesthood, its offerings, its furniture, its arrangement—all are symbolic of CHRIST and the believer's approach to God through Christ.

(1) The brazen Altar stands for atonement by blood.

(2) The Laver of Cleansing stands for Sanctification through the "washing of water by the Word."

(3) The Table of Shew Bread, is a type of Christ the food and strength of His people.

(4) The Golden Candlestick, with its seven branches, is a type of Christ the Light of the world.

(5) The Altar of Incense represents prayer and supplications that ascend to the throne of God. (Cf. Rev. 8:3.)

(6) The Mercy Seat, in the holy of holies, represents Christ as the only means of Justification and Access to the Presence of God. (See Luke 18:13, where the publican's prayer, "God be merciful to me a sinner," can be paraphrased, "God, meet me at the Mercy Seat.")

(7) The ark, in the holy of holies, speaks of Christ, as our Representative and Mediator at the right hand of God. The ark was made of wood, covered with pure gold (Exod. 25:10, 11). This speaks to us of the humanity (wood) and the Deity (pure gold) of Christ. In the ark were three things: "the golden pot that had manna," "Aaron's rod that budded," and "the tables of the law." These speak to us in types and pictures, of Messiah as the Bread that came down from Heaven; of His resurrection; and of His perfect keeping of the law. In HIS heart alone the Law remains unbroken.

(8) The Tabernacle itself speaks to us of the Incarnation: Christ dwelling among His people (see John 1:14).

The boards, the sockets, the curtains, the coverings, EVERYTHING connected with the tabernacle and its service, is a type of CHRIST in some way or another.

The FEASTS OF THE LORD, in Leviticus 23, are a beautiful and progressive revelation of the work of Christ for His people and the unfolding of the plan of God, through Christ, especially as related to Israel.

And so the wondrous story of the TYPES in the Old Testament unfolds, giving us vast and understandable revelations of the coming Messiah, and of His Person and work.

Messianic typology in the Old Testament opens a door to the fuller comprehension of Messiah, the Christ of God. The book of Hebrews shows clearly that these amazing types in the Old Testament are NOT the result of mere chance, but were divinely planned to give us pictures of Christ and His offering on the cross (see Hebrews 5-10). Indeed, we are told that Moses, when about to construct the Tabernacle, was "admonished of God . . . to make all things according to the pattern showed him" (Heb. 8:5). In other words, GOD planned the types—lives of men, institutions like the tabernacle and its worship, and events in the history of Israel— to serve as illustrations and shadows "of heavenly things."

*   *   *   *
CONCLUSION
We believe we have conclusively shown that:

(1) Not only is there genuine prophecy in the Bible, and in the Bible alone, but that this prophecy (2) PROVES beyond all doubt that Jesus of Nazareth, the central character of the New Testament, is the predicted Messiah of the Old Testament; (3) that this Messiah (Christ) is GOD manifested in the flesh; (4) that the Bible is the Word of God; and (5) the God of the Bible is the only true God; and (6) that the salvation of man's soul depends entirely on trusting Christ and what He did on the cross as the Redeemer, for one's eternal salvation.

Moreover, since these great facts are not only true but PROVABLE, by the evidence produced in this book, it is the duty of each individual not only to trust Christ for salvation, but surrender to His Lordship and live for Him. Since the Bible tells us that man's eternal destiny depends on trusting Christ —"he that believeth on the SON hath everlasting life: and he that believeth not the Son shall not see life; but the wrath of God abideth on him" (John 3:36)—it should be our greatest desire to tell others these facts, and let them know that "there is none other Name under heaven given among men whereby we must be saved." (Acts 4:12).

"THESE ARE WRITTEN THAT YE MIGHT BELIEVE THAT JESUS IS THE CHRIST, THE SON OF GOD: AND THAT BELIEVING YE MIGHT HAVE LIFE (ETERNAL LIFE) THROUGH HIS NAME" (John 20:31).

CPSIA information can be obtained
at www.ICGtesting.com
Printed in the USA
BVHW030218041019
560238BV00001B/51/P

9 781614 272649